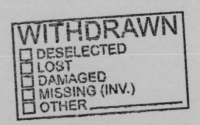

Shakespeare Studies

Monograph Series I

Shakespeare Studies Monograph Series

STUDIES IN THE BIBLIOGRAPHY OF
RENAISSANCE DRAMATIC TEXTS

I

Edited by
J. LEEDS BARROLL

Monograph I: THE "SHAKESPEAREAN"
ADDITION IN THE BOOKE OF SIR THOMAS
MOORE: SOME AIDS TO SCHOLARLY AND
CRITICAL SHAKESPEAREAN STUDIES
by
THOMAS CLAYTON

The Center for Shakespeare Studies
VANDERBILT UNIVERSITY
1969

WM. C. BROWN COMPANY PUBLISHERS
Dubuque, Iowa

Contents

I. GENERAL PREFACE

Et tu Shakespeare an diabolus—"to vary an old phrase which is penned in the margin of one of the other additions"—concluded the late R. C. Bald of the authorship and handwriting of Addition IIc in his thorough critical survey of *"The Booke of Sir Thomas More and Its Problems."*[1] And Harold Jenkins, also quoting Bald's conclusion, adds that "it is difficult to see what other verdict could be reached" in his cogent "Supplement to the Introduction" in the 1961 lithographic reproduction of Sir Walter Greg's edition of the play first printed by the Malone Society in 1911. By no means all the problems of *The Booke of Sir Thomas Moore* have been solved, especially the problem of the dates of its original composition and revision, or stages of revision, which have ranged from 1586 to 1605,[2] but Greg's assertion that the case for the identity of Shakespeare's otherwise known hand and that of Addition IIc "is stronger than any that has been made out for their being different"[3] remains valid forty years later. Indeed, it has been strengthened in that time and seems likely to remain as a case virtually proved, through the work of the scholars who have variously contributed to its establishment and support, most notably Richard Simpson, Samuel Spedding, Sir Edward Maunde Thompson, Greg himself, Alfred W. Pollard, J. Dover Wilson, R. W. Chambers, Caroline Spurgeon, R. C. Bald, and Harold Jenkins. And *Shakespeare's Hand in the Play of Sir Thomas More,* a collection of papers by Pollard, Greg, Maunde Thompson, Dover Wilson, and Chambers, is a monument of comprehensive scholarship: it is at once a formidable collective investigation carefully and convincingly conducted and something of an "instant anthology" of scholarly and critical models.

If *More* Addition IIc is indeed of Shakespeare's authorship and in his own handwriting,[4] its importance for the scholarly and critical study of many aspects of Shakespeare's text, style, manner of composition, and chronology can scarcely be exaggerated. But even if the Addition were not in Shakespeare's hand intensive re-examination of the manuscript would serve as the primary foundation for the establishment of a non-Shakespearean hypothesis. I was prompted to provide the present aids in the conviction that the Addition is Shakespeare's in both hand and authorship, but I hope that they will facilitate study of the Addition whatever hypothesis one holds or seeks.

I first gave close attention to the *More* Addition in pursuit of paleographical evidence to confute or support a proposed resolution of a textual crux,[5] and I soon discovered that it was no quick or easy matter to locate individual letters and similar groups of letters in the manuscript, and came to recognize the potential usefulness of an "Index Litterarum." A need for such an Index was already strongly implicit in the comments on the formation of individual letters, and real and potential paleographical ambiguities, made by—among others—Maunde Thompson in

Shakespeare's Handwriting and "The Handwriting of the Three Pages Attributed to Shakespeare Compared with His Signatures," and by Dover Wilson in "Bibliographical Links between the Three Pages and the Good Quartos" (*Shakespeare's Hand*, pp. 57-112 and 113-131). Since I had been occasionally engaged in related work with computers, it occurred to me that an Index Litterarum might be provided by the computer with minimal human effort and manual labor—which, along with the total cost and the time required, I underestimated, as is frequently the case with preliminary computational fantasies. I decided that I should also provide a Concordance and an "Orthographical Index Verborum," the latter alphabetically to record in full the evidence from which, for example, Dover Wilson made his selection for the "Appendix" on "The Spellings of the Three Pages, with Parallels from the Quartos," in which he cites parallels in twenty-nine classes of significant spelling-variants (*Shakespeare's Hand*, pp. 132-141). These aids and a few supplementary ones, with the texts from which the aids have been prepared, are provided below.[6]

Since all aspects of *The Booke of Sir Thomas Moore* are discussed in detail in works noted in the list of Abbreviations, it will be sufficient for the present purpose to provide a condensed description of the identity and distribution of the hands and the Additions in the manuscript, which is, of course, British Museum Harleian MS. 7368. The text proper of *The Booke* as it is presently bound occupies twenty leaves and thirty-seven pages, that is, folios 3-22^r (ff. 6^v and 9^v are blank), which were written in six different hands; a seventh hand is that of Edmund Tilney, Master of the Revels, "who, as censor, made certain notes and alterations and is probably also responsible for a few marginal marks" (Greg, "Handwritings," p. 41). Greg designated the six hands as S (because he first thought it the hand of a scribe) and A-E. The hands "are now assigned as follows, though with varying degrees of confidence" (Jenkins, p. 180): S to Anthony Munday, A to Henry Chettle, B to Thomas Heywood, C to an anonymous playhouse-bookkeeper, D to Shakespeare, and E to Thomas Dekker.[7] According to the hypothesis generally accepted at present, *The Booke* is a collaborate play, for which S, "Munday, as one of the part-authors, had undertaken the responsibility of fitting together the composite material and providing a fair copy" (Bald, p. 47) and in which D's—Shakespeare's (?)—share consisted solely in acting as a late expert consultant, as it were, in "producing an entirely new version of a portion of scene vi originally written by the same author as scene iv" (Greg, "Handwriting," p. 47), that is, Addition IIc, and perhaps in being the author of the twenty-one lines of Addition III, which is in C's hand.

Detailed accuracy is impossible of economical attainment with a book as bibliographically complicated as *Moore*, and the following details are to be understood as suggestive approximations only. What survives of the "original" manuscript (that is, Munday's fair-copy) constitutes the major part of the manuscript in its present state (twenty-five of thirty-seven pages), but some of Munday's pages have been altered by additions, revisions, and markings for deletion, and some revised pages have been inserted. Roman numerals—and lower-case letters—are customarily assigned to eight Additions, which constitute the major revisions. Addition I, in Chettle's hand (A) on folio 6^r (f. 6^v is blank), was wrongly inserted where it is now bound (see Greg, "Handwritings," p. 42, and Bald, p. 46). Addition IIa, in Heywood's or at any rate B's hand, on folio 7^r, is an expanded version of a short scene on folio 5^v marked for deletion. Addition IIb, in C's hand on folio 7^v, consists of a complete scene "continuing the elaborate composite insertion begun by B" as Addition IIa (Greg, "Handwritings," p. 44) and an initial stage-direction for the revised part of Scene VI beginning, without its own stage-direction, on folio 8^r, the first of the "Three Pages" of IIc.

Addition IIc, the subject of the present work, is in D's, presumably Shakespeare's, hand and occupies folios 8-9^r. Of the original part-scene revised in these pages only three lines—in Munday's hand and marked for omission—survive, on folio 10^r (f.9^v is blank). The twenty-one-line soliloquy of Addition III, in C's hand but quite possibly of Shakespeare's authorship, was formerly pasted over the lower part of folio 11^v. C wrote most of Addition IV (ff.12-13), but Dekker (E) added a few words on upper, and a closing episode on lower, folio 13^v. Addition V, in C's hand, contains a single eighteen-line speech that was once pasted over the lower part of folio 14^r; an eight-line preparation for it is written vertically in the left margin of both the original and the scrap of the Addition.[8] Addition VI, in B's (Heywood's?) hand, occupies folio 16; it is an episode intended to be inserted where a scene concludes in the middle of folio 17^r and is of interest in that fifteen lines on folio 16^r were obviously deleted by the author-scribe himself.

Simplified as it is, this brief description should suggest the complexity and authorial and paleographical variegation of *The Booke* and afford some of the evidence that Shakespeare is most unlikely to have had a hand in the original collaboration. But the text of Addition IIc—especially when compared with the fragment of the original by another—is also sufficient to confer clear distinction upon "D (Shakespeare?)" even if he "was never anything but a reviser" (Bald, p. 47). And it is worth adding Greg's comment on D's work: "It is without question the hand of an author composing as he writes, probably with great fluency. The writing is in some respects careless and impatient: speakers' names are omitted or miswritten, and in one place, after complicated alteration and deletion [ll. 112-114], the passage was left in such a tangled state as to call for C's intervention" ("Handwriting," p. 45). D's speech-prefixes are indeed an instructive study in idiosyncracy and indifference in such matters: "Lincoln," for example, is spelled and abbreviated in four different ways, and the casual "other" in three.

ABBREVIATIONS

Bald   R. C. Bald, "*The Booke of Sir Thomas More* and Its Problems," *ShS*, II (1949), 44-65 (the source of reference here); reprinted in *Evidence for Authorship: Essays on Problems of Attribution*, ed. David V. Erdman and Ephim G. Fogel (Ithaca, New York, 1966), pp. 146-175.

Greg	W. W. Greg, "Special Transcript of the Three Pages," *Shakespeare's Hand,* pp. 228-229 and [230-242].
Greg, "Handwritings"	W. W. Greg, "The Handwritings of the Manuscript," *Shakespeare's Hand,* pp. 41-56.
Greg, *More*	*The Book of Sir Thomas More,* ed. W. W. Greg (Oxford: Malone Society, 1911; reprinted, with two minor corrections and a "Supplement" by Harold Jenkins, 1961).
Greg, *IMD*	"[Ill May Day Scenes From] The Booke of Sir Thomas Moore," ed. W. W. Greg, *Shakespeare's Hand,* pp. 193-227.
Jenkins	Harold Jenkins, "Supplement to the Introduction," *The Book of Sir Thomas More,* ed. W. W. Greg (Oxford, repr. 1961); reprinted in Malone Society *Collections VI* (Oxford, 1961 [1962]), 179-192 (the source of reference here).
Jenkins, *More*	Modern-spelling edition of *Sir Thomas More,* ed. Harold Jenkins, in *William Shakespeare: The Complete Works,* ed. C. J. Sisson (London, 1954), pp. 1238-66 (Addition IIc, pp. 1245-47).
Maunde Thompson	Sir Edward Maunde Thompson, *Shakespeare's Handwriting* (Oxford, 1916).
Shakespeare's Hand	*Shakespeare's Hand in The Play of Sir Thomas More,* ed. A. W. Pollard (Cambridge, England, 1923).

FACSIMILES AND TRANSCRIPTIONS USED

Books	Facsimiles	Transcriptions
Tudor Facsimile Texts, ed. John S. Farmer (n.p., 1910)	Entire manuscript	None
Greg, *More* (1911)	Ll. 96-123, between pp. xxxi and 1	Entire manuscript; IIc, pp. 73-78
Maunde Thompson (1916)	Addition IIc, 3 pls. between pp. 32 and 33	IIc, pp. 32-37
†*Shakespeare's Hand* (1923)	Ll. 72-87 and 126-140, before p. 67	IIc, pp. [230-242]
Bald (1949)	Addition IIc, pls. XIII-XV	IIc, pp. 62-65
Evidence for Authorship (1966; reprint of Bald)	Addition IIc, pls. 1-3	IIc, pp. 172-175

†*References to Greg's transcription of Addition IIc are to that contained here unless otherwise specified.*

Contractions. In the Concordance and Orthographical Index Verborum, conventional compound-contractions (e.g., "we'll") are treated and counted as one word. Unconventional compound-contractions (in modern terms)—"BYTH'," "TH'APOSTLE," "TH'ART," "TH'HIP," "TH'OFFENDER," and "TOTH'"—are so listed and counted as one each in the Orthographical Index but (except for "-TH'") cross-referenced by the second segment; in the Concordance they are listed and counted by their segments. The effect of this difference in treatment on total counts is small: the total number of *different* words remains the same; the total number of words is two more in the Concordance (where separate "ART" and "TH'" increase "BY" and "TO" by one each).

Counts (Absolute Frequencies). Wherever counts are given for items in indexes and lists, they are given in the margin to the left of the item to which they apply. Counts for subordinate entries are included in the total count of the corresponding major entry.

Deletions. [ ] Deletions in the manuscript are enclosed between square brackets (so Bald, Greg in *More,* and Maunde Thompson; in Greg's transcription in *Shakespeare's Hand,* deletions are scored through by overprinting); they are D's own deletions except as otherwise noted in the critical apparatus to the texts.

Distributions and Statistics. For reasons of space there is no "character concordance" (though More himself does most of the talking), and, while some statistical information likely to be of general interest is provided, much that might be of use to some persons is not. For example, I have not given separate counts for the occurrences of words in verse and in prose contexts, respectively; the relative frequencies of variant spellings (though they are obvious in approximation); or, in the Concordance itself, relative frequencies for each word (these are given, however, in the Frequency List that follows the Concordance). Few statistics are entirely innocent of distortions attendant upon necessary exercises of judgment, for the reason that is but choosing can rarely be found not to have slight but significant—and legitimate—alternatives; the inherent limitations of the comparatively few statistics provided will be understood, I am sure, by those who consult them.

Doubtful Points of Transcription. Words and letters conjecturally transcribed are differentiated by *italics* in directly-printed text and by underscoring in text photo-offset-reproduced from computer-printed text (Bald and Maunde Thompson use pointed, and Greg square, brackets). The comparatively few doubtful points of transcription (in all, twenty-one) *are* included in the total number of words and other statistics given below. They are (modernized): *A,* article (2: ll. 1 & 3), *AT* (l. 2), AUTHORITY (l. 94b), *BE* (l. 4), *EVEN* (l. 46), *GOD* (l. 95b), *IT* (l. 147b), *LIST* (l. 3), *MEAL* (l. 2), NOBLES, sb. (coins) (l. 3), *ONE* (l. 62), *POUND* (l. 2), *RED* (l. 1), *STONE,* sb. (l. 3), STRANGERS (l. 4), SUFFERED (l. 4), SURREY (l. 48), THE (l. 17), US (l. 18), and WATCHINS (l. 43).[9] In the Concordance, the doubtful words have separate, appropriately underscored headwords, with which they are grouped (and counted) below the group about which there is no doubt, or in the normal alphabetical sequence if there is only one occurrence. In the Orthographical Index, the underscored words constitute separate subordinate entries for the headword to which they belong (and in whose marginal total-counts theirs are included).

Headwords. These are given in modern-American spelling for all words for which there are "legitimate" modern equivalents. Several special cases require comment, however. Three manuscript forms, *argo, pumpions,* and *shrevaltry,* which have been modernized in the modern-spelling text, are headed "ERGO," "PUMPKINS," AND "SHRIEVALTY" elsewhere. The interlinear "prenty" (l. 22) is headed "PRENTICE" in the Orthographical Index Verborum simply to set it by itself by limited if inevitably licentious grouping in modern terms; "PRENTICES," the grouping in the Concordance, was almost certainly intended. Since D spelled *on* for both *on* and *one,* it is impossible to be sure which of two *on*'s in line 87 — "woold feed on on another" — should be regarded as "ONE" (v. Greg, *IMD,* p. 212, l.102n); with Jenkins's *More* I have read the second so, though our texts differ in another instance of MS. *on* (see note on Modern-Spelling Texts below, p. 77). In the verse-line 115, "as muty$\overset{n}{e}$s ar incident, by his name," I have taken *muty$\overset{n}{e}$s* as D's intending *mutnyes,* but misplacing the at-first-omitted *n,* and treated it is "MUTINIES" (so too Jenkins's *More).*[10] Not without hesitation I have followed Jenkins in interpreting and heading D's *how,* in line 28, as "HO," but *momtanish* (l. 140) is unfathomable to all: one has little choice but to reproduce it *literatim* in a conservative text, and I have headed the one occurrence "MOMTANISH."[11]

Homographs. These are grouped and counted as separate words. I have of course exercised my own judgment in assigning words to their categories, and some words — of which there are examples s.v. "HEADWORDS" above — are clearly open to alternative interpretation and description. When two or more words orthographically identical (in modern spelling) but grammatically different occur, each is differentiated by a lower-case "discriminant" immediately following the headword; the abbreviations (e.g., "a." for "adjective") are obvious and standard, and homographic groups are ordered alphabetically according to the spelling of the discriminant. Where only one form of a homograph occurs, explicit discrimination (e.g., "MARK, v.") is given only where the form might mislead. I have made allowance for the reader's awareness that he is dealing with Elizabethan English (hence "ARTHUR" seems to me to need no following "personal name," though most names have it), but I cannot be sure that I have not overlooked a few words that perhaps should have been identified.

Line-numbers. The line-numbers are those of the standard twentieth-century facsimiles and transcriptions of Addition IIc, except that here line 38.1 is so distinguished, as it is by being on a separate line in the manuscript, from line 38 proper, with which it is customarily numbered in transcriptions; and lines 94, 95, 114, and 147 — as 94a and 94b, &c. — are printed and referred to as pairs of lines, as they inferentially are in literary intention, though they are written as single lines in the manuscript (ll. 114b and 147b are half-lines; ll. 94 and 95 were written as one pair rather than two pairs presumably so that they could be fitted in at the bottom of f. 8^v).

Speech-prefixes. D's prefixes are included *literatim* in the transcription and the Index Litterarum, and most, expanded and in modern spelling, are retained in the modern-spelling text (those abandoned there in favor of the prefixes of the "final revision" as touched up by C are recorded in the critical apparatus). D's prefixes are not included in the Concordance or in the Orthographical Index Verborum, but a separate Index to them precedes the latter.

II. THE ELIZABETHAN TEXT

The transcription might be described more accurately as a "critical conflation," since I have not been able to examine the manuscript at first hand. But I have collated the transcriptions of Bald, Greg, and Maunde Thompson, and Jenkins's corrections of the transcription given in Greg's *More* ("Supplement," pp. 191-192), and carefully compared every reading of the transcriptions with the facsimiles under the highest practical magnification. The resulting transcription has, I think, generally high reliability, and it will not surprise, as I cheerfully acknowledge, that it is nearly identical with Greg's last one (1923) and that where it is not I have felt some sense of *hubris*. "Major" differences in transcription—they are not very major—are recorded in the critical apparatus and commented on where necessary. Maunde Thompson gives detailed, and Greg very detailed, descriptive and analytical notes. Like Bald, Greg, and Maunde Thompson, I retain the horizontal rules that— not quite consistently—separate speeches by different characters. I have normalized *I/J* as *I* (Greg uses *J*) and modernized to *s* the Secretary ſ's—which Greg retains—that are used invariably by D for the minuscule letter in initial and medial positions.

The symbols for manuscript-abbreviations in the transcription, indexes, and list are either more or less standard or (in computer-printed text, when they differ) as near like the manuscript forms as the available characters permitted (peculiarities in the "alphabetical" treatment of special characters are discussed in the headnote to the Index Litterarum below). They are the tittle (typographically a tilde, as in õ), which indicates "omission of an *m* or *n* at the end of a word or syllable; for this, the tittle is placed over the letter preceding the omitted letter,"[12] and here also the omission of other letters, notably terminal -*er* in *eu~* (*eu@* in computer-printed text) and medial -*ies*- in *ma[ies]t̃ie*. The others are p̲, that is, "p" underscored (p̲), for *par*- and *per*-; ꝑ (ꝑ) for *pro*-; and ꝫ (standard; ¬ in computer-printed text) for terminal -*s*, -*es*, -*is* (Bald normalizes the latter as *s*). Boldface type is used in the transcription to indicate C's alterations and additions in Addition IIc.

F. 8r

5

10

15

20

14

Lincolne

Peace heare me, he that will not see a red hearing at a harry
grote, butter at a levenpence a pounde, meale at nyne shillinge a
Bushell and Beeff at fower nobles a stone, lyst to me

[other] **Geo bett**

yt will Come to that passe yf straingers be sufferd mark him

Linco

our Countrie is a great eating Country, argo they eate more in
our Countrey then they do in their owne

[other] **betts clow**

by a half penny loff a day troy waight

Linc

they bring in straing rootes, which is meerly to the vndoing of poor
prentizes, for whatp [a watrie] a sorry psnyp to a good hart

[oth] **willian**

trash trash,: they breed sore eyes and tis enough to infect the
Cytty wt the palsey

Lin

nay yt has infected yt wt the palsey, for theise basterde of dung
as you knowe they growe in Dvng haue infected vs, and yt is our
infeccion will make the Cytty shake which ptly Coms through
the eating of psnyps

[o] **Clown • betts**
Enter
seriant

trewe and pumpions togeather

what say you to the mercy of the king do you refuse yt

Lin

you woold haue vs vppon thipp woold you no marry do we not, we
accept of the kinge mercy but wee will showe no mercy vppõ
the straingers

seriaunt   youᵘ ar the simplest thinge that eu~ stood in such a question

Lin   now prenty
       how say you prentisses symple downe wᵗʰ him

all   prentisses symple prentisses symple
                Enter the L maier Surrey
                        Shrewsbury

[Sher] **Maior**   hold in the kinge name hold

Surrey
mayer   frende masters Countrymen
         peace how peace I [sh] Charg you keep the peace

Shro   my masters Countrymen

[Sher] **Williamson**   The noble Earle of Shrewsbury lette hear him

Ge bette   weele heare the Earle of Surrey

Linc   the earle of Shrewsbury

bette   weele heare both

25

30

Addition IIc (Transcription). *B = Bald, G = Greg, T = Maunde Thompson; s.p. = speech-prefix; ∧ = a wanting point, and ~ = the substantive of the lemma* (10) *s.p.* willian] *B;* william *G, T (both note that m has two minims only)* (16) *s.p.* Clown] *G;* ~. *T;* ~, *B* (17) *s.p.* seriant] *G. T;* Seriant *B (a misprint: cf. Bald, p. 55)* the] *B;* the *G, T;* the *is probably right, but part of the word is obscured by a pasteover* (22) *Greg: "The marginal and interlined words were added later" (p. [231], l. 22n)* (24) L∧] *G, T;* L. *B* (30),(32) Shrewsbury] *G;* Shrowsbury *B,* Greg in More, *T*

15

16

all	both both both both	
Linc	Peace I say peace ar you men of Wisdome [ar] or what ar you	35
Surr	[But] what you will haue them but not men of wisdome	
all	weele not heare my L of Surrey, [all] no no no no no	
	Shrewsbury shr	38.1
moor	whiles they ar ore the banck of their obedyenc thus will they bere downe all thinge	40
Linc	Shreiff moor speakes shall we heare shreef moor speake	
Doll	Lette heare him a keepes a plentyfull shrevaltry· and a made my Brother Arther watchins Seriant Safes yeoman lete heare shreeve moore	45
all	Shreiue moor moor more Shreue moore	
moor	even by the rule you haue among yor sealues Comand still audience	F. 8v
all	Surrey Sury	
all	moor moor	
Lincolne bette	peace peace scilens peace·	50
moor	You that haue voyce and Credyt wt the [mv] nvmber Comaund them to a stilnes	

		55
		60
		65
		70

Lincolne   a plaigue on them they will not hold their peace the deule
Cannot rule them

moor   Then what a rough and ryotous charge haue yoᵘ
to Leade those that the deule Cannot rule
good masters heare me speake

Doll   I byth mas will we moor thart a good howskeeper and I
thanck thy good worship for my Brother Arthur watchins

all   peace peace

moor   look what yoᵘ do offend yoᵘ Cry vppõ
that is the peace; not on of yoᵘ heare present
had there such fellowes lyvd when yoᵘ wer babes
that ċoold haue topt the peace, as nowe you woold
the peace wherin yoᵘ haue till nowe growne vp
had bin tane from yoᵘ, and the bloody tymes
coold not haue brought yoᵘ to [theise] the state of men
alas poor thingꝭ what is yt yoᵘ haue gott
although we graunt yoᵘ geat the thing you seeke

[D] Bett   marry the removing of the straingers wᶜʰ cannot choose but
much [helpe] advauntage the poor handycraftes of the Cytty

moor   graunt them remoued and graunt that this yoʳ [y] noyce
hath Chidd downe all the matie of Ingland

(42) shrevaltry•] ∼ T; ∼, B, G   (46) even] G, T; even B   (50) peace•] ∼. B; ∼∧ G, T (55) s.p. moor] G, T; ∼. B; ∼∧ G, T; Moor B

17

18

ymagin that you see the wretched straingers
their babyes at their backe, [and]wt their poor lugage
plodding tooth porte and coste for transportacion
and that you sytt as kinge in your desyres
aucthoryty quyte sylenct by yor braule
and you in ruff of yor [yo] opynions clothd
what had you gott; Ile tell you, you had taught
how insolenc and strong hand shood prevayle
how orderd shood be quelld, and by this patterne
not on of you shoold lyve an aged man
for other ruffians as their fancies wrought
wth sealf same hand sealf reasons and sealf right
woold shark on you and men lyke ravenous fishes
woold feed on on another

Doll   before god thate as trewe as the gospell

Bette lincoln   nay this a sound fellowe I tell you lets mark him

moor   Let me sett vp before yor thoughts good freinde
on supposytion, which if you will marke
you shall pceaue howe horrible a shape
your ynnovation beres, first tis a sinn
which oft thappostle did forwarne vs of vrging obedienc to aucthoryty
and twere [in] no error yf I told you all   you wer in armes gainst god

all   marry god forbid that

moo   nay certainly you ar
for to the king god hath his offyc lent

of dread of Iustyce, power and Comaund
hath bid him rule, and wild yoᵘ to obay
and to add ampler maͭie to this
he [god] hath not [le] only lent the king his figure
&
his throne [his] sword, but gyven him his owne name
calls him a god on earth, what do yoᵘ then
rysing gainst him that god himsealf enstalls
but ryse gainst god, what do yoᵘ to yoʳ sowles
in doing this o desperat [ar] as you are·
wash your foule mynds wᵗ teares and those same handᵉ
that yoᵘ lyke rebells lyft against the peace
lift vp for peace, and your vnreuerent knees
[that] make them your feet   to kneele to be forgyven
[is safer warrs, then euer yoᵘ can make]
      [in in to yoʳ obedienc·]
[whose discipline is ryot;] [why euen yoʳ warrs hurly]
tell me but this
[cannot ᵽceed but by obedienc] what rebell captaine
  ⁿn
as mutyes ar incident, by his name

(75) [and] wᵗ] G; omit wᵗ B, T; Greg: "and was crossed out, and wᵗ interlined to replace it, by D" (p. [236], l. 75n)   lugage] B, T; lugᵍage G (82) orderd] G, T; ordere B; Greg: "M[ore] ordere: doubtful, but in either case an error for order" (p. [237], l. 82n) (93) your]G, T; yoʳ B; Greg: "the reading though indistinct is hardly open to question" (p. [237], l. 93n) (103) &] G, T; omit B; Greg: "The & is really written on the top of his not between the lines" (p. [239], l. 103n)   (107) are·] G; ~. T; ~ᴧB (112-114) Greg: "With the exception of the single word warrs (which he crossed out, adding hurly in its place) these lines were left standing by D. All the other deletions are in darker ink, presumably by C, who added the interlined words [tell me but this]" (p. [239], ll. 112-4n); also see Greg's note on these lines in the critical apparatus for the modern-spelling text of IIc (l. 144)   (113) ryot;] G, T; ~, B   obedienc·] G; ~ᴧ B, T (115) mutyes] G; mutynes B, T; the reading as Greg transcribes it is very clear, but the n presumably should have been put before the y (see General Notes above, s.v. "Headwords")

can still the rout who will obay [th] a traytor
or howe can well that ꝓclamation sounde
when ther is no adicion but a rebell
to quallyfy a rebell, youle put downe straingers 120
kill them cutt their throts possesse their howses
and leade the matie of lawe in liom

[alas alas]
to slipp him lyke a hound; [sayeng] say nowe the king
as he is clement,. yf thoffendor moorne 125
shoold so much com to short of your great trespas
as but to banysh you, whether woold you go•
what Country by the nature of yoᵣ error
shoold gyve you harber go you to ffraunc or flanders
to any larman ꝓvince, [to] spane or portigall 130
nay any where [why you] that not adheres to Ingland
why you must needɇ be straingers, woold you be pleasd
to find a nation of such barbarous temper
that breaking out in hiddious violence
woold not afoord you, an abode on earth 135
whett their detested knyves against yoᵣ throtes
spurne you lyke dogge, and lyke as yf that god
owed not nor made not you, nor that the elamentɇ

yoᵣ
wer not all appropriat to [their] Comforte•
but Charterd vnto them, what woold you thinck 140
to be thus vsd, this is the straingers case
and this your momtanish inhumanyty

all

fayth a saies trewe letts [vs] do as we may be doon by

[all] **Linco**

weele be ruld by you master moor yf youle stand our
freind to ₚcure our ᵽdon

moor   145

Submyt you to theise noble gentlemen
entreate their mediation to the kinge
gyve vp yoʳ sealf to forme obay the maiestrate
and thers no doubt, but mercy may be found   yf you so seek yt

(122) [alas alas]] *Greg: "The substituted words, interlined by D, were deleted by C" (p. [241], l. 122n)* hound;] G, T; ~, B (123) cle-ment,] G; ~, B, T; *Greg: "there seems clearly to be a point" after the comma (p. [241], l. 123n)* 125 go•] G; ~. T; ~ₐ B (141) letts [vs]] *Greg, ascribing the deletion to C, suggests that "the writer probably intended lett vs but forgot to cross out the s" (p. [241], l. 141n)* (147) yt] *omit T*

21

ii. Orthographical Indexes

1. *Index to the Punctuation.* The punctuation of hand D is indexed and counted separately before the Index Verborum.

2. *Orthographical Index to the Speech-Prefixes.* The speech-prefixes of hand D are indexed and counted separately before the Index Verborum.

3. *Orthographical Index Verborum.* The words of Addition IIc are grouped alphabetically under appropriate headwords in modern-American spelling, with multiple homographs given in alphabetical order according to their identifying words or abbreviations. Line-numbers begin immediately after the headword (and supplementary information, if any) if *all* occurrences of the word are *both* identical and entirely minuscule in the manuscript (and, therefore, the typographical inverse of the fully capitalized headword): thus "2 THAT, a. (4, 117)" means that both occurrences are of the form *that* in the manuscript. Subordinate listings are given whenever an occurrence differs *in any way* from the exact typographical inverse of the headword (except that "1 BYTH' (58)" = MS. *byth*), as in

1 LET, v.

1 Let (90).

The order of subordinate listings is alphabetical (as modified by the accommodation of not strictly alphabetical characters); capitalized forms are given before words (present or hypothetical) that are otherwise identical: thus, s.v. "LET'S, comp. contr.," are "let¬, lets, Lett¬, lett¬, letts."

For unconventional compound-contractions, see *Aids* (p. 11), s.v. *"Contractions."*

4. *Variant Spellings.* The words of multiple occurrence spelled in more than one way in Addition IIc are given, with the variants, in a list following the Index Verborum.

(a) Index to the Punctuation

38	COMMA,	1, 2, *2, 3,* 5, 8, 9, 10 (,:), 12, 13, 18, 38, 64, 66, 75, 80, 82, 91, 93, 99, 100, 103, 104, 106, 110, 112, 115, 119, 123 (,•), 125, 128, 130, 133, 135, 136, 138, 139, 147
4	SEMI-COLON;	62, 80, 113, 122 (all as •,)
1	COLON:	10 (,:)
7	PERIOD.	42, 50, 107, 113, 123 (,.), 125, 137 (all are located well above the base-line)

(b) Orthographical Index to the Speech-Prefixes

There are forty-nine speech-prefixes in hand D. They are spelled and located as follows.

10 ALL (23, 34, 38, 45, 48, 49, 60, 96, 140, 142)

1 Bettę (89)
3 bettę (31, 33, 50)

5 BETTS
    1 Bett ([D] Bett) (70)

3 DOLL
    3 Doll (42, 58, 88)

22

11 LINCOLN
    3 Lin (12, 18, 22)
    4 Linc (8, 32, 35, 41)
    1 Linco (5)
    3 Lincolne (1, 50, 53)

1 MAYOR
    1 mayer (28)

8 MORE
    1 moo (97)
    7 moor (39, 46, 51, 55, 61, 72, 144)

4 OTHER
    1 o (16)
    1 oth (10)
    2 other (4, 7)

2 SERGEANT
    1 seriant (17)
    1 seriaunt (21)

1 SHERWIN
    1 Sher (30)†

2 SHREWSBURY
    1 Sher (26)†
    1 Shro• (29)

2 SURREY
    1 Surr (37)
    1 Surrey (27)

† Greg remarks of *Sher* in l. 26, replaced by *Maior* by C, that it is "clearly an error, perhaps for *Shre*[*wsbury*]," and of *Sher* in l. 30, replaced by *williamson* by C, that as "*Sher*[*win*]" it "was clearly intentional" (*IMD*, pp. 209, ll. 35n and 39n [sic]).

26 A, article
24 a (1, 2, 2, 5, 7, 7, 9, 9, 9, 9,
   21, 42, 52, 53, 55, 58, 89,
   92, 93, 104, 116, 118, 119,
   122, 131)
2 a (1, 3)

3 A, pron. (see also "HE") (42, 42,
   141)

1 ABODE, sb. (133)

1 ACCEPT (19)

1 ADD (101)

1 ADDITION
1 adicion (118)

1 ADHERES (129)

1 ADVANTAGE, v.
1 advauntage (71)

1 AFFORD
1 afoord (133)

2 AGAINST (see also "'GAINST") (109,
   134)

1 AGED (83)

3 ALAS (68, 122, 122)

5 ALL (38, 40, 73, 95, 137)

1 ALTHOUGH (69)

1 AMONG (46)

1 AMPLER (101)

2 AN (83, 133)

29 AND
1 & (103)
28 and (3, 10, 13, 16, 42, 51, 55,
   58, 66, 72, 75, 76, 77, 79,
   81, 82, 85, 86, 95, 99, 100,
   101, 108, 110, 121, 135, 140,
   147)

1 ANOTHER (87)

1 ANY (128)

1 ANYWHERE
1 any where (129)

APOSTLE (see "TH'APOSTLE")

1 APPROPRIATE, ppl. a. (137)

9 ARE
8 ar (21, 35, 35, 36, 39, 97, 107,
   115)
1 are (107)

1 ARMS, sb.
1 armes (95)

ART, v. (BE; see "TH'ART")

2 ARTHUR
1 Arther (43)
1 Arthur (59)

12 AS (13, 64, 77, 84, 88, 88, 107,
   115, 123, 125, 135, 141)

5 AT
4 at (1, 2, 3, 75)
1 at (2)

1 AUDIENCE (47)

2 AUTHORITY
1 aucthoryty (78)
1 aucthoryty (94)

1 AYE
1 I (58)

1 BABES (63)

1 BABIES
1 babyes (75)

24

1 BACKS, sb.
1 back¬ (75)

1 BANISH
1 banysh (125)

1 BANK
1 banck (39)

1 BARBAROUS (131)

1 BASTARDS
1 basterd¬ (12)

9 BE
8 be (82, 111, 130, 130, 139, 141, 142, 147)
1 <u>be</u> (4)

1 BEAR, v.
1 bere (40)

1 BEARS, v.
1 beres (93)

1 BEEF
1 Beeff (3)

1 BEEN
1 bin (66)

2 BEFORE (88, 90)

1 BID, v. (100)

1 BLOODY (66)

5 BOTH (33, 34, 34, 34, 34)

1 BRAWL, sb.
1 braule (78)

1 BREAKING (132)

1 BREED, v. (10)

1 BRING (8)

2 BROTHER
2 Brother (43, 59)

1 BROUGHT (67)

1 BUSHEL
1 Bushell (3)

2 BUT, adv. (37, 125)

7 BUT, conj.
1 But (37)
6 but (19, 70, 103, 106, 138, 147)

2 BUT, prep. (114, 118)

1 BUTER (2)

9 BY (7, 46, 78, 82, 114, 115, 126, 141, 142)

1 BYTH' (58)

1 CALLS, v. (104)

3 CAN (112, 116, 117)

4 CANNOT
2 Cannot (54, 56)
2 cannot (70, 114)

1 CAPTAIN
1 captaine (114)

1 CASE, sb. (139)

1 CERTAINLY (97)

1 CHARGE, sb. (55)

1 CHARGE, v.
1 Charg (28)

1 CHARTERED
1 Charterd (138)

1 CHID
1 Chidd (73)

1 CHOOSE (70)

3 CITY
  3 Cytty (11, 14, 71)

1 CLEMENT (123)

1 CLOTHED
  1 clothd (79)

1 COASTS, sb.
  1 cost¬ (76)

2 COME
  1 com (124)
  1 Come (4)

1 COMES
  1 Coms (14)

1 COMFORTS, sb.
  1 Comfort¬ (137)

1 COMMAND, sb.
  1 Comaund (99)

2 COMMAND, v.
  1 Comand (47)
  1 Comaund (52)

2 COULD
  2 coold (64, 67)

4 COUNTRY
  1 Countrey (6)

COUNTRY
  1 Countrie (5)
  2 County (5, 126)

2 COUNTRYMEN
  2 Countrymen (27, 29)

1 CREDIT, sb.
  1 Credyt (51)

1 CRY, v.
  1 Cry (61)

1 CUT, v.
  1 cutt (120)

1 DAY (7)

1 DESIRES, sb.
  1 desyres (77)

1 DESPERATE (107)

1 DETESTED (134)

2 DEVIL
  2 deule (53, 56)

1 DID (94)

1 DISCIPLINE, sb. (113)

7 DO (6, 17, 18, 61, 104, 106, 141)

1 DOGS, sb.
  1 dogg¬ (135)

1 DOING (107)

1 DONE
  1 doon (141)

1 DOUBT, sb. (147)

4 DOWN
  4 downe (22, 40, 73, 119)

1 DREAD, sb. (99)

2 DUNG
  1 dung (12)
  1 Dvng (13)

3 EARL
  2 Earle (30, 31)
  1 earle (32)

2 EARTH (104, 133)

1 EAT
  1 eate (5)

2 EATING (5, 15)

26

1 ELEMENTS, sb.
  1 element¬ (136)

1 ELEVENPENCE
  1 a levenpence (2)

2 ENGLAND
  2 Ingland (73, 129)

1 ENOUGH (10)

1 ENTER
  1 Enter (24)

1 ENTREAT
  1 entreate (145)

1 ERGO
  1 argo (5)

2 ERROR (95, 126)

2 EVEN, emphatic particle
  1 euen (113)
  1 euen (46)

2 EVER
  1 eua (21)
  1 euer (112)

1 EYES, sb. (10)

1 FAITH, interj.
  1 fayth (141)

1 FANCIES, sb. (84)

1 FEED (87)

1 FEET (111)

1 FELLOW
  1 fellowe (89)

1 FELLOWS
  1 fellowes (63)

1 FIGURE, sb. (102)

1 FIND (131)

1 FIRST (93)

1 FISHES, sb. (86)

1 FLANDERS (127)

4 FOR, conj. (9, 12, 84, 98)

3 FOR, prep. (59, 76, 110)

1 FORBID (96)

1 FORGIVEN
  1 forgyven (111)

1 FORM, sb.
  1 forme (146)

1 FORWARN
  1 forwarne (94)

1 FOUL
  1 foule (108)

1 FOUND (147)

1 FOUR
  1 fower (3)

1 FRANCE
  1 ffraunc (127)

1 FRIEND
  1 freind (143)

2 FRIENDS
  1 freind¬ (90)
  1 frend¬ (27)

1 FROM (66)

3 'GAINST (see also "AGAINST")
  3 gainst (95, 105, 106)

1 GENTLEMEN (144)

1 GERMAN
  1 Iarman (128)

3 HE (see also "A, pron.") (1, 102, 123)

9 HEAR
1 hear (30)
8 heare (1, 31, 33, 38, 41, 42, 43, 57)

1 HEART
1 hart (9)

1 HELP, v.
1 helpe (71)

1 HERE
1 heare (62)

1 HERRING
1 hearing (1)

1 HIDEOUS
1 hiddious (132)

10 HIM (4, 22, 30, 42, 89, 100, 103, 104, 105, 122)

1 HIMSELF
1 himsealf (105)

HIP (see "TH'HIP")

6 HIS (98, 102, 103, 103, 103, 115)

1 GROW
1 growe (13)

1 GROWN
1 growne (65)

4 HAD (63, 66, 80, 80)

1 HALFPENNY
1 half penny (7)

2 HAND (81, 85)

1 HANDICRAFTS
1 handycraftes (71)

1 HANDS
1 hand- (108)

1 HARBOR
1 harber (127)

1 HARRY, sb. as a. (1)

1 HAS (12)

4 HATH (73, 98, 100, 102)

10 HAVE
10 haue (13, 18, 37, 46, 51, 55, 64, 65, 67, 68)

1 GET
1 geat (69)

2 GIVE
2 gyve (127, 146)

1 GIVEN
1 gyven (103)

2 GO (125, 127)

9 GOD
8 god (88, 96, 98, 102, 104, 105, 106, 135)
1 god (95)

5 GOOD, a. (9, 57, 58, 59, 90)

1 GOSPEL
1 gospell (88)

2 GOT
2 gott (68, 80)

3 GRANT, v.
3 graunt (69, 72, 72)

2 GREAT (5, 124)

1 GROAT
1 grote (2)

1 HO
   1 how (28)

3 HOLD, v. (26, 26, 53)

1 HORRIBLE (92)

1 HOUND, sb. (122)

1 HOUSEKEEPER
   1 howskeeper (58)

1 HOUSES, sb.
   1 howses (120)

5 HOW
   3 how (22, 81, 82)
   2 howe (92, 117)

1 HURLY (113)

5 I
   5 I (28, 35, 58, 89, 95)

7 IF
   1 if (91)
   6 yf (4, 95, 123, 135, 142, 147)

1 I'LL, comp. contr.
   1 Ile (80)

1 IMAGINE
   1 ymagin (74)

15 IN (5, 6, 8, 13, 21, 26, 77, 79, 95, 95, 107, 113, 113, 121, 132)

1 INCIDENT, a. (115)

1 INFECT (10)

2 INFECTED (12, 13)

1 INFECTION
   1 infeccion (14)

1 INHUMANITY
   1 inhumanyty (140)

1 INNOVATION
   1 ynnovation (93)

1 INSOLENCE (81)

1 INSTALLS
   1 enstalls (105)

10 IS (5, 8, 13, 62, 68, 112, 113, 118, 123, 139)

7 IT
   6 yt (4, 12, 12, 13, 17, 68)
   1 Yt (147)

1 JUSTICE
   1 Iustyce (99)

1 KEEP (28)

1 KEEPS
   1 keepes (42)

1 KILL (120)

5 KING
   4 king (17, 98, 102, 122)
   1 kinge (145)

2 KING'S, sing. poss.
   2 king⌐ (19, 26)

1 KINGS, sb.
   1 king⌐ (77)

1 KNEEL
   1 kneele (111)

1 KNEES (110)

1 KNIVES
   1 knyves (134)

1 KNOW
   1 knowe (13)

1 LAW
   1 lawe (121)

2 LEAD, v. (līd)
   1 Leade (56)

1 LEAD, v. (līd)
1 leade (121)

2 LENT, v. (98, 102)

1 LET, v.
1 Let ,90)

5 LET'S, comp. contr.
1 let¬ (43)
1 lets (89)
1 lett¬ (42)
1 lett¬ (30)
1 letts (141)

2 LIFT
1 lift (110)
1 lyft (109)

5 LIKE, adv.
5 lyke (86, 109, 122, 135, 135)

1 LIST, v. (=LISTEN)
1 lyst (3)

1 LIVE, v.
1 lyve (83)

1 LIVED
1 lyvd (63)

1 LOAF
1 loff (7)

1 LOOK (61)

2 LORD
2 L (24, 38)

1 LUGGAGE
1 lugage (75)

1 LYAM
1 liom (121)

2 MADE (42, 136)

1 MAGISTRATE
1 maiestrate (146)

3 MAJESTY
1 matie (101)
2 matie (73, 121)

3 MAKE (14, 111, 112)

1 MAN (83)

3 MARK, v.
2 mark (4, 89)
1 marke (91)

3 MARRY, interj. (18, 70, 96)

1 MASS, sb. (oath) (58)

1 MASTER, sb. (142)

3 MASTERS, sb. (27, 29, 57)

2 MAY, v. (141, 147)

1 MAYOR
1 maier (24)

4 ME (1, 3, 57, 90)

1 MEAL
1 meale (2)

1 MEDIATION (145)

4 MEN (35, 37, 67, 86)

4 MERCY (17, 19, 19, 147)

1 MERELY
1 meerly (8)

1 MINDS
1 mynds (108)

1 MOMTANISH (140)

1 MORE, a. (5)

11 MORE, personal name
8 moor (41, 41, 45, 45, 49, 49,
58, 142)

30

MORE, personal name
2 moore (44, 45)
1 more (45)

1 MOURN
1 moorne (123)

2 MUCH (71, 124)

1 MUST (130)

1 MUTINIES, sb.
1 muty̅es (115)

4 MY (29, 38, 42, 59)

3 NAME, sb. (26, 103, 115)

1 NATION (131)

1 NATURE (126)

4 NAY (12, 89, 97, 129)

1 NEEDS, adv.
1 need¬ (130)

1 NINE
1 nyne (2)

10 NO (18, 19, 38, 38, 38, 38, 38, 95, 118, 147)

2 NOBLE, a. (30, 144)

1 NOBLES, sb. (coins)
1 nobles (3)

1 NOISE
1 noyce (72)

2 NOR (136, 136)

14 NOT (1, 18, 37, 38, 53, 62, 67, 83, 102, 129, 133, 136, 136, 137)

4 NOW
1 now (22)
3 nowe (64, 65, 122)

1 NUMBER, sb.
1 nvmber (51)

1 O (107)

4 OBEDIENCE
3 obedienc (94, 113, 114)
1 obedyenc (39)

3 OBEY
3 obay (100, 116, 146)

1 O'ER
1 ore (39)

26 OF (8, 12, 15, 17, 19, 30, 31, 32, 35, 37, 38, 39, 62, 67, 70, 71, 73, 79, 83, 94, 99, 99, 121, 124, 126, 131)

1 OFFEND (61)

OFFENDER (see "TH'OFFENDER")

1 OFFICE
1 offyc (98)

1 OFT (94)

6 ON (53, 86, 87, 91, 104, 133)

3 ONE
2 on (83, 87)
1 on (62)

1 ONLY (102)

1 OPINIONS
1 opynions (79)

4 OR (35, 117, 127, 128)

1 ORDER
1 orderd (82)

1 OTHER (84)

5 OUR (5, 6, 13, 142, 143)

1 OUT (132)

1 OWED (136)

2 OWN, a.
  2 owne (6, 103)

2 PALSEY (11, 12)

1 PARDON, sb.
  1 pdon (143)

1 PARSNIP
  1 psnyp (9)

1 PARSNIPS
  1 psnyps (15)

1 PARTLY
  1 ptly (14)

1 PASS, sb.
  1 passe (4)

1 PATTERN
  1 patterne (82)

7 PEACE, sb. (28, 53, 62, 64, 65, 109, 110)

10 PEACE, v. (interj.)
  2 Peace (1, 35)
  8 peace (28, 28, 35, 50, 50, 50, 60, 60)

1 PERCEIVE
  1 pceaue (92)

1 PLAGUE
  1 plaigue (53)

1 PLEASED
  1 pleasd (130)

1 PLENTIFUL
  1 plentyfull (42)

1 PLODDING (76)

4 POOR (8, 68, 71, 75)

1 PORTS
  1 port¬ (76)

1 PORTUGAL
  1 portigall (128)

1 POSSESS
  1 possesse (120)

1 POUND
  1 pounde (2)

1 POWER (99)

1 PRENTICE
  1 prenty (22)

4 PRENTICES
  3 prentisses (22, 23, 23)
  1 prentizes (9)

1 PRESENT, a. (62)

1 PREVAIL
  1 prevayle (81)

1 PROCEED
  1 pceed (114)

1 PROCLAMATION
  1 pclamation (117)

1 PROCURE
  1 pcure (143)

1 PROVINCE
  1 pvince (128)

1 PUMPKINS
  1 pumpions (16)

1 PUT (119)

1 QUALIFY
  1 quallyfy (119)

1 QUELLED
   1 quelld (82)

1 QUESTION, sb. (21)

1 QUITE
   1 quyte (78)

1 RAVENOUS (86)

1 REASONS, sb. (85)

3 REBEL, sb.
   3 rebell (114, 118, 119)

1 REBELS, sb.
   1 rebells (109)

1 RED
   1 red (1)

1 REFUSE, v. (17)

1 REMOVED
   1 remoued (72)

1 REMOVING (70)

1 RIGHT, sb. (85)

1 RIOT, sb.
   1 ryot (113)

1 RIOTOUS
   1 ryotous (55)

1 RISE
   1 ryse (106)

1 RISING
   1 rysing (105)

1 ROOTS, sb.
   1 rootes (8)

1 ROUGH (55)

1 ROUT, sb. (116)

1 RUFF (79)

1 RUFFIANS (84)

1 RULE, sb. (46)

3 RULE, v. (54, 56, 100)

1 RULED
   1 ruld (142)

1 SAFER (112)

1 SAFE'S, personal name, poss.
   1 Safes (43)

1 SAME (108)

4 SAY (17, 22, 35, 122)

1 SAYING
   1 sayeng (122)

1 SAYS
   1 saies (141)

2 SEE (1, 74)

2 SEEK
   1 seek (147)
   1 seeke (69)

2 SELF
   2 sealf (85, 85)

1 SELFSAME
   1 sealf same (85)

1 SERGEANT
   1 Seriant (43)

1 SET, v.
   1 sett (90)

1 SHAKE (14)

2 SHALL (41, 92)

1 SHAPE, sb. (92)

1 SHARK, v. (86)

1 SHILLINGS
   1 shilling‑ (2)

1 SHORT (124)

5 SHOULD
   5 shoold (81, 82, 83, 124, 127)

1 SHOW, v.
   1 showe (19)

5 SHREWSBURY, personal name
   1 shr (38.1)
   4 Shrewsbury (25, 30, 32, 38.1)

1 SHRIEVALTY
   1 shrevaltry (42)

5 SHRIEVE
   1 shreef (41)
   1 shreeve (44)
   1 shreiff (41)
   1 shreiue (45)
   1 shreue (45)

1 SILENCE, v. (interj.)
   1 scilens (50)

1 SILENCED
   1 sylenct (78)

3 SIMPLE
   3 symple (22, 23, 23)

1 SIMPLEST (21)

1 SIN, sb.
   1 sinn (93)

1 SIT
   1 sytt (77)

1 SLIP
   1 slipp (122)

2 SO (124, 147)

1 SORE, a. (10)

1 SORRY (9)

1 SOULS
   1 sowles (106)

1 SOUND, a. (89)

1 SOUND, v.
   1 sounde (117)

1 SPAIN
   1 spane (128)

2 SPEAK
   2 speake (41, 57)

1 SPEAKS
   1 speakes (41)

1 SPURN
   1 spurne (135)

1 STAND, v. (142)

1 STATE, sb. (67)

1 STILL, a. (47)

1 STILL, v. (116)

1 STILLNESS
   1 stilnes (52)

1 STONE, sb.
   1 stone (3)

1 STOOD (21)

1 STRANGE
   1 straing (8)

6 STRANGERS
   5 straingers (20, 70, 74, 119, 130)
   1 straingers (4)

1 STRANGERS'
1 straingers (139)

1 STRONG (81)

1 SUBMIT
1 Submyt (144)

3 SUCH (21, 63, 131)

1 SUFFERED
1 sufferd (4)

1 SUPPOSITION
1 supposytion (91)

5 SURREY, personal name
3 Surrey (24, 31, 38)
1 Surrey (48)
1 Sury (48)

1 SWORD (103)

1 TAKEN
1 tane (66)

1 TAUGHT (80)

1 TEARS, sb.
1 teares (108)

2 TELL (80, 89)

1 TEMPER, sb. (131)

2 THAN
2 then (6, 112)

1 THANK
1 thanck (59)

1 TH'APOSTLE
1 thappostle (94)

1 TH'ART
1 thart (58)

2 THAT, a. (4, 117)

5 THAT, conj. (72, 74, 77, 135, 136)

12 THAT, pron. (1, 21, 51, 56, 62, 64, 96, 105, 109, 111, 129, 132)

1 THAT'S, comp. contr.
1 that¬ (88)

46 THE
1 The (30)
44 the (8, 10, 11, 12, 14, 15, 17, 19, 20, 21, 24, 26, 28, 31, 32, 39, 46, 51, 53, 56, 62, 64, 65, 66, 67, 69, 70, 70, 71, 71, 73, 74, 88, 98, 102, 109, 116, 121, 122, 126, 136, 139, 145, 146)

THE
1 the (17)

12 THEIR (6, 39, 53, 75, 75, 75, 84, 120, 120, 134, 137, 145)

8 THEM (37, 52, 53, 54, 72, 111, 120, 138)

2 THEN
1 Then (55)
1 then (104)

2 THERE
1 ther (118)
1 there (63)

1 THERE'S
1 thers (147)

3 THESE
3 theise (12, 67, 144)

8 THEY (5, 6, 8, 10, 13, 39, 40, 53)

1 TH'HIP
1 thipp (18)

1 THING (69)

3 THINGS
3 thing¬ (21, 40, 68)

1 THINK
  1 thinck (138)

1 THIS, a. (82)

5 THIS, pron. (72, 101, 107, 139, 140)

1 THIS, pron.; comp. contr. (89)

1 TH'OFFENDER
  1 thoffendor (123)

2 THOSE (56, 108)

1 THOUGHTS (90)

2 THROATS
  1 throtes (134)
  1 throts (120)

1 THRONE (103)

1 THROUGH (14)

2 THUS (40, 139)

1 THY (59)

1 TILL (65)

1 TIMES
  1 tymes (66)

2 'TIS
  2 tis (10, 93)

32 TO (3, 4, 8, 9, 10, 17, 52, 56, 67, 94, 98, 100, 101, 101, 106, 111, 111, 113, 119, 122, 125, 127, 128, 128, 129, 131, 137, 139, 143, 144, 145, 146)

1 TOGETHER
  1 togeather (16)

1 TOLD (95)

1 TOO (124)

1 TOPPED
  1 topt (64)

1 TOTH'
  1 tooth (76)

1 TRAITOR
  1 traytor (116)

1 TRANSPORTATION
  1 transportacion (76)

2 TRASH, sb. (10, 10)

1 TRESPASS, sb (124)

1 TROY (7)

1 TRUE, a.
  1 trewe (88)

2 TRUE, adv.
  2 trewe (16, 141)

1 'TWERE
  1 twere (95)

1 UNDOING, vbl. sb.
  1 vndoing (8)

1 UNREVERENT
  1 vnreuerent (110)

1 UNTO
  1 vnto (138)

4 UP
  4 vp (65, 90, 110, 146)

3 UPON
  2 vppõ (19, 61)
  1 vppon (18)

1 URGING
  1 vrging (94)

4 US
  3 vs (13, 94, 141)
  1 vs (18)

1 USED
  1 vsd (139)

1 VIOLENCE (132)

1 VOICE
  1 voyce (51)

2 WARS
  2 warrs (112, 113)

1 WASH, v. (108)

2 WATCHINS, personal name
  1 watchins (59)
  1 watchins (43)

1 WATERY
  1 watrie (9)

7 WE
  6 we (18, 18, 41, 58, 69, 141)
  1 wee (19)

1 WEIGHT
  1 waight (7)

4 WE'LL
  4 weele (31, 33, 38, 142)

1 WELL (117)

3 WERE (63, 95, 137)

12 WHAT (17, 36, 37, 55, 61, 68, 80, 104, 106, 114, 126, 138)

1 WHAT'S, comp. contr.
  1 what⌐ (9)

2 WHEN (63, 118)

1 WHEREIN
  1 wherin (65)

1 WHET
  1 whett (134)

5 WHICH
  1 w^{ch} (70)
  4 which (8, 14, 91, 94)

1 WHILES (39)

1 WHITHER
  1 whether (125)

1 WHO (116)

1 WHOSE (113)

3 WHY (113, 129, 130)

10 WILL, v. (1, 4, 14, 19, 37, 40, 53, 58, 91, 116)

1 WILLED
  1 willd (100)

2 WISDOM
  1 Wisdome (35)
  1 wisdome (37)

7 WITH
  5 w^t (11, 12, 51, 75, 108)
  2 wth (22, 85)

1 WORSHIP, sb. (59)

9 WOULD
  9 woold (18, 18, 64, 86, 87, 125, 130, 133, 138)

1 WRETCHED (74)

1 WROUGHT, v. (84)

1 YEOMAN (43)

59 YOU
  1 Yo^u (51)
  55 yo^u (17, 17, 18, 18, 21, 22, 28, 35, 36, 37, 46, 55, 61, 61, 62, 63, 64, 65, 66, 67, 68, 69, 69, 74, 77, 79, 80, 80, 80, 83, 86, 89, 91, 92, 95, 95, 97, 100, 104, 106, 109, 112, 125, 125, 127, 129, 130, 130, 133, 135, 136, 138, 142,

Of the 164 words in D's hand that occur more than once, thirty-two (19.5%) are spelled in more than one way (excluding as variants capitalized forms, as such, and two special cases, "dung/Dvng" and "euen/even").

29	AND	1 &, 28 and (& is an interlinear addition)
9	ARE	8 ar, 1 are
2	ARTHUR	Arther, Arthur
2	COME	com, Come
3	COMMAND	2 Comaund (1 sb. and 1 v.), 1 Comand (v.)
4	COUNTRY	1 Countrey, 1 Countrie, 2 Country
2	EVER	eu~ , euer
2	FRIENDS	freinde, frende
9	HEAR	1 hear, 8 heare
5	HOW	3 how, 2 howe
7	IF	1 if, 6 yf
5	KING	4 king, 1 kinge
5	LET'S	lete, lets, Lette, lette, letts
2	LIFT	lift, lyft
3	MAJESTY	2 matie, 1 matie
3	MARK	2 mark, 1 marke
11	MORE (name)†	8 moor, 2 moore, 1 more
4	NOW	1 now, 3 nowe
4	OBEDIENCE	3 obedienc, 1 obedyenc
4	PRENTICES	3 prentisses, 1 prentizes (on *prenty* see p. 12)
2	SEEK	seek, seeke
5	SHREWSBURY†	1 shr, 4 Shrewsbury
5	SHRIEVE	shreef, shreeve, Shreiff, Shreiue, Shreue
5	SURREY†	4 Surrey, 1 Sury
2	THERE	ther, there
2	THROATS	throtes, throts
3	UPON	2 vppõ, 1 vppon
7	WE	6 we, 1 wee
5	WHICH	1 wch, 4 which
7	WITH	5 wt, 2 wth
59	YOU	1 You, 55 you, 3 you
17	YOUR	10 yor, 7 your

†See also Index to Speech-Prefixes (above).

iii. Index Litterarum

The Index Litterarum is a concordance of letters. It has several peculiarities, owing both to the paleographical vagaries of the text and to the logic of such an index. The special alphabet of the Index consists (here) of twenty-four standard letters (there is no *J* for paleographical reasons, and *X* does not occur) and seven special symbols, which as *subject*-characters occur in separate groups before *A*. Each of the thirty-one characters is hypothetically listed in four classes (not all of which occur for every character): "SOLITARY," "INITIAL," "MEDIAL," and "TERMINAL." The subject-character is given in six vertical columns per page and indicated at the top of each column by an asterisk (*); the other letters of the word are given at the right and left of the subject-character as they occur in the word, according to the rules for each of the three multiple-character groupings.

The "SOLITARY" grouping is self-explanatory (see, e.g., "&, SOLITARY" and "*A*, SOLITARY"). "INITIAL" words are listed in alphabetical order, with all words beginning with capitals listed before the first of the words beginning with a lower-case (minuscule) letter; in fact, capitalized words always occur before corresponding uncapitalized words within an overall alphabetical sequence. "TERMINAL" characters are alphabetized from *right to left*, beginning at the character to the left of the subject-character. "MEDIAL" entries are alphabetized, first, by the letter to the *left* of the subject-character; second, by the letter to the *right* of the subject-character; third, by the remaining characters to the left, running from *right to left*; and, last, by the remaining letters to the right, running from *left to right*. This last set of rules is admittedly complicated, but it is the means by which similar medial paleographical-groups are brought together in relation to a particular subject-character.

The seven special characters—in the order in which they occur in their separate groups at the head of the alphabet—are:

Printed Character	Paleographical Character	Letters Abbreviated, &c.	Alphabetical Treatment
&, SOLITARY	&	*and*	Pre-alphabetical
@, TERMINAL	~	*-er*	As *-er*, but see further comments
ᵱ, INITIAL	ᵱ	*par-, per-*	As *p-a-r-*
ꝑ, INITIAL	ꝑ	*pro-*	As *p-r-o-*
¬, TERMINAL	ℯ	*-s*	As though between *r* and *s*
õ, TERMINAL	õ	*-on*	See comments below
ĩ, MEDIAL	ĩ	*-ies-*	See comments below

It is more economical and helpful to explain what happens to the few occurrences of @, õ, and ĩ (when they are merely part of the context of another subject-character) than to explain in programming terms why it happens.[13] For @ (only in *eu@*, i.e., "euer"), the order s.v. "*E*, INITIAL" is *eu@*, *euen*, *euer*, *eyes*; s.v. "*U*, MEDIAL" it is *euen*, *euer*, *Shreue*, *vnreuerent*, *eu@*, *deule*. For õ, the order is *vppõ*, *vppõ*, *vppon* s.v. "*V*, INITIAL" and — for the first *p*—"*P*, MEDIAL"; but *vppon*, *vpp̃o*, *vpp̃o* for the second "P, MEDIAL." As for t̃, the order is *matie*, *mãtie*, *matie* s.v. "E, TERMINAL" and "M, INITIAL," but *mãtie*, *mãtie*, *p̃clãmation*, *mãtie*, *Comãund* s.v. "A, MEDIAL": *matie* occurs a number of entries after *matie*, *matie* s.v. "I, MEDIAL."

Paleographical Alternates: I/J, U/V. Between *I* and *J* no distinction is made in the manuscript, and none is made here: *I* and *i* have been used throughout. Under "I, INITIAL" *Iarman* and *Iustice* would be *phonetically* transliterated as *J*-words, as, under "I, MEDIAL," would *maiestrate*, *Seriant*, *seriant*, and *seriaunt*.

There are no majuscule "INITIAL" forms of either *U* or *V* in the Addition, and the paleographical distinctions have been maintained for all the minuscule forms. As one would expect, "V, INITIAL" is used exclusively as the initial form for both *u* and *v*; of seventeen occurrences, all but two (*violence* and *voyce*) would be phonetically transliterated as *u*. As for paleographical "U, MEDIAL," of twenty-one occurrences representing *v* all but four (*eu@*, *deule* [twice], and *sealues*) fall between standard vowels. Of the twelve occurrences of "V, MEDIAL" two (*Dvng* and *nvmber*), both between standard consonants, represent phonetic *u*, the remaining ten *v*. An ostensible "V, TERMINAL" (l. 51), *mv*, is in fact a false start for *nvmber*, which was written immediately after *mv*. Hand D generally uses paleographical *u* for phonetic *v* in medial positions (20)—in -*aue* (11), -*eue*- (4), -*eu@* (1), -*eul*- (2), -*iue* (1), and -*oue*- (1), but he sometimes uses paleographical for phonetic *v* (7)—in -*ave*- (1), -*eva*- (2), -*eve* and -*eve*- (2), -*ova*- (1), and -*ovi*- (1), as well as after *D*, *d*, *n*, *p̨*, and *y*.

Superscript Letters. Superscript letters, as *subject*, are listed after all occurrences of the subject-letter not written superscript; thus, s.v. "H, TERMINAL," the last four entries are *byth*, *wᶜʰ*, *wᵗʰ*, *wᵗʰ*. When they are not the subject, they follow special rules. If they immediately precede or follow the subject-letter, they are *grouped* after the *groups* of words—present or hypothetical—with which they are otherwise identical (thus the *yoᵘ*'s follow the *you*'s s.v. "O, MEDIAL"). When they fall in other positions, they are treated as identical with the same letter not written superscript, and the two forms are intermixed (thus, s.v. "Y, INITIAL," *you* and *yoᵘ* are intermixed, being given in the numerical order in which they occur in the manuscript).

Truncated Words. Because of the compression due to the printing of six columns per page, a few long words are truncated at one end or the other in some contexts, a circumstance that has relatively little practical effect; as an extreme example, *transportacion* reads *sportacion* s.v. "N, TERMINAL."

Underscoring. Letters underscored *in the* entries are those conjecturally transcribed; they are alphabetized normally (by the rules), *following*, however, words identical except for the underscoring. Underscored letters are *not* included as subject-letters, but a list of words (with line-number references) conjecturally transcribed in whole or in part is given in the note on Doubtful Points of Transcription above (p. 11). The subject-letter *heading*, e.g., "<u>A</u>, INITIAL," is underscored solely for emphasis.

ε, SOLITARY
*
ε 103

ə, TERMINAL
*
euə 21

p, INITIAL
*
pɔeaue 92   pdon 143

p, INITIAL
*
pceed 114   pclamation 11   pcure 143   pvince 128   psnyp 9   psnyps 15   ptly 14

r, TERMINAL
*
need¬ 130   dogg¬ 135   king¬ 26   what¬ 9   cost¬ 76   Lett¬ 42
hand¬ 108   thing¬ 21   king¬ 77   let¬ 43   Bett¬ 89   lett¬ 30
frend¬ 27   thing¬ 40   shilling¬ 2   elament¬ 136   bett¬ 31
freind¬ 90   thing¬ 68   back¬ 75   Comfort¬ 137   bett¬ 33
basterd¬ 12   king¬ 19   that¬ 88   port¬ 76   bett¬ 50

õ, TERMINAL
*
vppõ 19   vppõ 61

t̃, MEDIAL
*
m̃atie 101

42

A, SOLITARY

*	*	*	*	*	*
a 1	a 7	a 21	a 53	a 93	a 122
a 2	a 7	a 42	a 55	a 104	a 131
a 2	a 9	a 42	a 58	a 116	a 141
a 2	a 9	a 42	a 89	a 118	
a 5	a 9	a 52	a 92	a 119	

A, INITIAL

*	*	*	*	*	*
Arther 43	all 38	an 133	and 85	ar 35	as 115
Arthur 59	all 38	and 3	and 86	ar 35	as 123
abode 133	all 40	and 10	and 95	ar 36	as 125
accept 19	all 45	and 13	and 99	ar 39	as 135
add 101	all 48	and 16	and 100	ar 97	as 141
adheres 129	all 49	and 42	and 101	ar 107	at 1
adicion 118	all 60	and 51	and 108	ar 115	at 2
advauntage 71	all 73	and 55	and 110	are 107	at 3
afoord 133	all 95	and 58	and 121	argo 5	at 75
against 109	all 96	and 66	and 135	armes 95	aucthoryty 78
against 134	all 137	and 72	and 140	as 13	aucthoryty 94
aged 83	all 140	and 75	and 147	as 64	audience 47
alas 68	all 142	and 76	another 87	as 77	
alas 122	although 69	and 77	any 128	as 84	
alas 122	among 46	and 79	any 129	as 88	
all 23	ampler 101	and 81	appropriat 13	as 88	
all 34	an 83	and 82	ar 21	as 107	

A, MEDIAL

*	*	*	*	*	*
babes 63	barbarous 131	obay 146	Cannot 54	case 139	peace 28
babyes 75	barbarous 131	calls 104	Cannot 56	day 7	peace 28
back¬ 75	basterd¬ 12	can 112	cannot 70	Peace 1	peace 35
banck 39	obay 100	can 116	cannot 114	Peace 35	peace 50
banysh 125	obay 116	can 117	captaine 114	peace 28	peace 50

43

A, MEDIAL

*	*	*	*	*	*	*
peace 50	heare 42	shall 92	that 1	that 109	seriant 17	marry 96
peace 53	heare 43	hand 81	that 4	that 111	Iarman 128	mas 58
peace 60	heare 57	hand 85	that 21	that 117	mediation 145	master 142
peace 60	heare 62	hand- 108	that 51	that 129	appropriat 137	masters 27
peace 62	hearing 1	handycraftes 7	that 56	that 132	seriaunt 21	masters 29
peace 64	teares 108	thanck 59	that 62	that 135	plaigue 53	masters 57
peace 65	pleasd 130	shape 92	that 64	that 136	Cpclamation 117	matie 73
peace 109	reasons 85	thappostle 94	that 72	that- 88	elament- 136	matie 121
peace 110	eate 5	harber 127	that 74	what 17	flanders 127	Cpclamation 117
Leade 56	eating 5	harry 1	that 77	what 36	Ingland 73	matie 101
leade 121	eating 15	hart 9	that 96	what 37	Ingland 129	Comaund 52
dread 99	geat 69	Charg 28	that 105	what 55	alas 68	Comaund 99
speake 41	togeather 16	charge 55		what 61	alas 122	may 141
speake 57	great 5	Charterd 138		what 68	alas 122	may 147
speakes 41	great 124	shark 86		what 80	lawe 121	mayer 28
breaking 132	entreate 145	thart 58		what 104	made 42	name 26
sealf 85	pceaue 92	has 12		what 106	made 136	name 103
sealf 85	fancies 84	hath 73		what 114	ymagin 74	name 115
sealf 85	fayth 141	hath 98		what 126	maier 24	nation 131
sealf 146	lugage 75	hath 100		what 138	maiestrate 146	nature 126
sealues 46	gainst 95	hath 102		what- 9	make 14	nay 12
himsealf 105	gainst 105			haue 13	make 111	nay 89
Earle 30	gainst 106			haue 18	make 112	nay 97
Earle 31	against 109			haue 37	man 83	nay 129
earle 32	against 134			haue 46	Comaund 47	palsey 11
earth 104	portigall 128			haue 51	yeoman 43	palsey 12
earth 133	had 63			haue 55	Iarman 128	spane 128
hear 30	had 66			haue 64	inhumanyty 140	passe 4
heare 1	had 80			haue 65	mark 4	trespas 124
heare 31	had 80			haue 67	mark 89	patterne 82
heare 33	shake 14			haue 68	marke 91	handycraftes 71
heare 38	half 7			ruffians 84	marry 18	straing 8
heare 41	shall 41			Seriant 43	marry 70	straingers 20

44

A, MEDIAL

*	*	*	*	*	*
straingers 70	desperat 107	sayeng 122	safer 112	state 67	warrs 113
straingers 74	maiestrate 146	transportacion 76	Safes 43	taught 80	forwarne 94
straingers 119	braule 78	advauntage 71	saies 141	quallyfy 119	wash 108
straingers 130	ffraunc 127	captaine 114	same 85	shrevaltry 42	watchins 59
straingers 139	graunt 69	certainly 97	same 108	ynnovation 93	watchins 43
straingers 4	graunt 72	enstalls 105	say 17	advauntage 71	watrie 9
transportacion	graunt 72	tane 66	say 22	prevayle 81	
trash 10	ravenous 86	momtanish 140	say 35	waight 7	
trash 10	traytor 116	stand 142	say 122	warrs 112	

B, INITIAL

*	*	*	*	*	*
banysh 125	Beeff 3	both 34	before 88	but 70	by 78
barbarous 131	Bett 70	both 34	before 90	but 103	by 82
basterd- 12	Bett- 89	both 34	bere 40	but 106	by 114
be 82	Brother 43	both 34	beres 93	but 114	by 115
be 111	Brother 59	braule 78	bett- 31	but 118	by 126
be 130	Bushell 3	breaking 132	bett- 33	but 125	by 141
be 130	But 37	breed 10	bett- 50	but 138	by 142
be 139	babes 63	bring 8	bid 100	but 147	byth 58
be 141	babyes 75	brought 67	bin 66	butter 2	
be 142	back- 75	but 19	bloody 66	by 7	
be 147	banck 39	but 37	both 33	by 46	

B, MEDIAL

*	*	*	*	*	*
babes 63	rebell 119	obedyenc 39	obay 116	harber 127	Shrewsbury 38.1
abode 133	rebells 109	noble 30	obay 146	forbid 96	Submyt 144
babyes 75	horrible 92	noble 144	obedienc 94	shrewsbury 25	doubt 147
rebell 114	nvmber 51	nobles 3	obedienc 113	shrewsbury 30	
rebell 118	obay 100	barbarous 131	obedienc 114	shrewsbury 32	

C, INITIAL

*	*	*	*	*	*
Cannot 54	Comaund 99	Country 126	Cytty 71	captaine 114	com 124
Cannot 56	Come 4	Countrymen 27	calls 104	case 139	coold 64
Charg 28	Comfort- 137	Countrymen 29	can 112	certainly 97	coold 67
Chatterd 138	Coms 14	Credyt 51	can 116	charge 55	cost- 76
Chidd 73	Countrey 6	Cry 61	can 117	choose 70	cutt 120
Comand 47	Countrie 5	Cytty 11	cannot 70	clement 123	
Comaund 52	Country 5	Cytty 14	cannot 114	clothd 79	

C, MEDIAL

*	*	*	*	*	*
accept 19	peace 60	infected 12	incident 115	pcure 143	such 21
Peace 1	peace 62	infected 13	banck 39	mercy 17	such 63
Peace 35	peace 64	which 8	thanck 59	mercy 19	such 131
peace 28	peace 65	which 14	thinck 138	mercy 19	aucthoryty 78
peace 28	peace 109	which 91	Linco 5	mercy 147	aucthoryty 94
peace 28	peace 110	which 94	Lincolne 1	scilens 50	noyce 72
peace 35	ransportacion 76	adicion 118	Lincolne 50	discipline 113	voyce 51
peace 50	back- 75	audience 47	Lincolne 53	watchins 59	Iustyce 99
peace 50	accept 19	violence 132	sylenct 78	watchins 43	handycraftes 71
peace 50	infeccion 14	levenpence 2	pceaue 92	wretched 74	ch
peace 53	infeccion 14	pvince 128	pceed 114	much 71	w 70
peace 60	infect 10	fancies 84	pclamation 117	much 124	

C, TERMINAL

*	*	*	*	*
obedienc 94	obedyenc 39	Linc 32	Linc 41	offyc 98
obedienc 113	Linc 8	Linc 35	ffraunc 127	
insolenc 81				

D, SOLITARY

*
D 70

D, INITIAL

*	*	*	*	*	*
Doll 42	desperat 107	did 94	do 61	doing 107	downe 73
Doll 58	desyres 77	discipline 11	do 104	doon 141	downe 119
Doll 88	detested 134	do 6	do 106	doubt 147	dread 99
Dvng 13	deule 53	do 17	do 141	downe 22	dung 12
day 7	deule 56	do 18	dogg¬ 135	downe 40	

D, MEDIAL

*	*	*	*	*	*
add 101	advauntage 71	need¬ 130	sounde 117	handycraftes 71	Wisdome 35
Leade 56	hiddious 132	obedyenc 39	thoffendor 123	plodding 76	Wisdome 37
leade 121	plodding 76	Credyt 51	vndoing 8	abode 133	audience 47
made 42	obedienc 94	hiddious 132	hand¬ 108	bloody 66	
made 136	obedienc 113	Chidd 73	frend¬ 27	pdon 143	
adheres 129	obedienc 114	incident 115	freind¬ 90	orderd 82	
adicion 118	mediation 145	flanders 127	mynds 108	basterd¬ 12	

D, TERMINAL

*	*	*	*	*
dread 99	remoued 72	shoold 83	and 10	Ingland 129
had 63	owed 136	shoold 124	and 13	Comand 47
had 66	clothd 79	shoold 127	and 16	stand 142
had 80	bid 100	woold 18	and 42	offend 61
had 80	forbid 96	woold 18	and 51	freind 143
add 101	did 94	woold 64	and 55	find 131
Chidd 73	quelld 82	woold 86	and 58	Comaund 52
Cceed 114	willd 100	woold 87	and 66	Comaund 99
feed 87	hold 26	woold 125	and 72	found 147
breed 10	hold 26	woold 130	and 75	hound 122
aged 83	hold 53	woold 133	and 76	sound 89
wretched 74	coold 64	woold 138	and 77	god 88
infected 12	coold 67	told 95	and 79	god 96
infected 13	shoold 81	ruld 142	and 81	god 98
detested 134	shoold 82	and 3	and 82	god 102
			Ingland 73	

D, TERMINAL

*	*	*	*	*
god 104	god 135	god 58	stood 21	Charterd 138	pleasd 130
god 105	god 9	god 59	orderd 82	aford 133	vsd 139
god 106	god 57	god 90	sufferd 4	sword 103	lyvd 63

E, INITIAL

*	*	*	*	*
Earle 30	earth 104	eating 15	entreate 145	euen 113
Earle 31	earth 133	element- 136	error 95	euer 112
Enter 24	eate 5	enough 10	error 126	eyes 10
earle 32	eating 5	enstalls 105	eu@ 21	

E, MEDIAL

	*	*	*	*	*
obedienc 94	bett- 50	seeke 69	fellowes 63	heare 38	theise 12
obedienc 113	pceaue 92	kneele 111	offend 61	heare 41	theise 67
obedienc 114	Cceed 114	weele 31	thoffendor 123	heare 42	theise 144
obedyenc 39	accept 19	weele 33	safer 112	heare 43	helpe 71
Beeff 3	certainly 97	weele 38	sufferd 4	heare 57	Bushell 3
before 88	incident 115	weele 142	Safes 43	heare 62	them 37
before 90	flanders 127	keep 28	geat 69	hearing 1	them 52
rebell 114	orderd 82	keepes 42	togeather 16	wretched 74	them 53
rebell 118	desperat 107	howskeeper 58	aged 83	their 6	them 54
rebell 119	desyres 77	meerly 8	gentlemen 144	their 39	them 72
rebells 109	detested 134	knees 110	straingers 20	their 53	them 111
bere 40	deule 53	feet 111	straingers 70	their 75	them 120
beres 93	deule 56	shreeve 44	straingers 74	their 75	them 138
nvmber 51	Cceed 114	infeccion 14	straingers 119	their 75	Then 55
harber 127	feed 87	infect 10	straingers 130	their 84	then 6
babes 63	need- 130	infected 12	straingers 139	their 120	then 104
Bett 70	breed 10	infected 13	hear 30	their 120	then 112
Bett- 89	Beeff 3	feed 87	heare 1	their 134	when 63
bett- 31	shreef 41	heare 1	heare 31	their 137	when 118
bett- 33	seek 147	fellowe 89	heare 33	their 145	adheres 129

E, MEDIAL

*

Sher 26
Sher 30
ther 118
there 63
thers 147
togeather 16
whether 125
other 4
other 7
other 84
another 87
Brother 43
Brother 59
Arther 43
where 129
wherin 65
fishes 86
whether 125
whett 134
they 5
they 6
they 8
they 10
they 13
they 39
they 40
they 53
obedienc 94
obedienc 113
obedienc 114
audience 47
maier 24
maiestrate 146

*

saies 141
fancies 84
keep 28
keepes 42
howskeeper 58
speakes 41
Leade 56
leade 121
pleasd 130
clement 123
gentlemen 144
lent 98
lent 102
scilens 50
violence 132
insolenc 81
plentyfull 42
sylenct 78
ampler 101
whiles 39
simplest 21
sowles 106
Let 90
let- 43
lets 89
Lett- 42
lett- 30
letts 141
levenpence 2
mediation 145
meerly 8
men 35
men 37

*

men 67
men 86
elament- 136
clement 123
gentlemen 144
Countrymen 27
Countrymen 29
mercy 17
mercy 19
mercy 19
mercy 147
armes 95
tymes 66
need- 130
kneele 111
knees 110
stilnes 52
Peace 1
Peace 35
peace 28
peace 28
peace 28
peace 35
peace 50
peace 50
peace 50
peace 53
peace 60
peace 60
peace 62
peace 64
peace 65
peace 109

*

peace 110
speake 41
speake 57
speakes 41
gospell 88
penny 7
levenpence 2
beres 93
adheres 129
present 62
temper 131
desperat 107
keepes 42
reasons 85
breaking 132
dread 99
great 5
great 124
entreate 145
rebell 114
rebell 118
rebell 119
rebells 109
Credyt 51
breed 10
shreef 41
shreeve 44
refuse 17
freind 143
freind- 90
Shreiff 41
Shreiue 45
remoued 72
removing 70
vnreuerent 110

*

frend- 27
prentisses 22
pren·isses 23
prentisses 23
prentizes 9
prenty 22
teares 108
beres 93
adheres 129
present 62
Seriant 43
seriant 17
seriaunt 21
desyres 77
wretched 74
Shreue 45
vnreuerent 110
shrevaltry 42
prevayle 81
Shrewsbury 25
Shrewsbury 30
Shrewsbury 32
Shrewsbury 38,1
trewe 16
trewe 88
trewe 141
Surrey 24
Surrey 27
Surrey 31
Surrey 38
Surrey 48
Countrey 6
sealf 85
sealf 85
sealf 85

*

sealf 146
sealues 46
himsealf 105
see 1
see 74
seek 147
seeke 69
present 62
Seriant 43
seriant 17
seriaunt 21
prentisses 22
prentisses 23
prentisses 23
possesse 120
howses 120
sett 90
palsey 11
palsey 12
teares 108
infected 12
infected 13
detested 134
tell 80
tell 89
temper 131
Enter 24
Charterd 138
basterd- 12
master 142
masters 27
masters 29
masters 57

E, MEDIAL

*	*	*	*	*	*
patterne 82	quelld 82	even 46	weele 31	wer 137	yeoman 43
butter 2	euen 113	levenpence 2	weele 33	fower 3	mayer 28
detested 134	euer 112	gyven 103	weele 38	power 99	babyes 75
andycraftes 71	vnreuerent 110	forgyven 111	weele 142	twere 95	eyes 10
rootes 8	sealues 46	knyves 134	well 117	fellowes 63	mutyes 115
throtes 134	question 21	owed 136	wer 63	sayeng 122	prentizes 9
remoued 72	ravenous 86	wee 19	wer 95	obedyenc 39	

E, TERMINAL

*	*	*	*	*	*
be 82	peace 109	he 102	the 62	the 146	kneele 111
be 111	peace 110	he 123	the 64	watrie 9	weele 31
be 130	audience 47	The 30	the 65	Countrie 5	weele 33
be 130	violence 132	the 8	the 66	matie 73	weele 38
be 139	levenpence 2	the 10	the 67	matie 101	weele 142
be 141	Qvince 128	the 11	the 69	matie 121	Ile 80
be 142	noyce 72	the 12	the 70	speake 41	symple 22
be 147	voyce 51	the 14	the 70	speake 57	symple 23
Peace 1	Iustyce 99	the 15	the 71	shake 14	symple 23
Peace 35	Leade 56	the 17	the 71	make 14	Earle 30
peace 28	leade 121	the 19	the 73	make 111	Earle 31
peace 28	made 42	the 20	the 74	make 112	earle 32
peace 28	made 136	the 21	the 88	seeke 69	thappostle 94
peace 35	sounde 117	the 24	the 98	marke 91	braule 78
peace 50	abode 133	the 26	the 102	lyke 86	deule 53
peace 50	see 1	the 28	the 109	lyke 109	deule 56
peace 50	see 74	the 31	the 116	lyke 122	foule 108
peace 53	wee 19	the 32	the 121	lyke 135	youle 119
peace 60	lugage 75	the 39	the 122	lyke 135	youle 142
peace 60	advauntage 71	the 46	the 126	le 102	rule 46
peace 62	kinge 145	the 51	the 136	horrible 92	rule 54
peace 64	charge 55	the 53	the 139	noble 30	rule 56
peace 65	he 1	the 56	the 145	noble 144	rule 100

E, TERMINAL

*	*	*	*	*	*
prevayle 81	Lincolne 53	heare 38	nature 126	haue 13	we 56
me 1	throne 103	heare 41	case 139	haue 18	we 69
me 3	forwarne 94	heare 42	theise 12	haue 37	we 141
me 57	patterne 82	heare 43	theise 67	haue 46	laue 121
me 90	moorne 123	heare 57	theise 144	haue 51	treve 16
name 26	spurne 135	heare 62	those 56	haue 55	treve 88
name 103	owne 6	bere 40	those 108	haue 64	treve 141
name 115	owne 103	there 63	whose 113	haue 65	howe 92
same 85	downe 22	where 129	choose 70	haue 67	howe 117
same 108	downe 40	twere 95	passe 4	haue 68	showe 19
Come 4	downe 73	ore 39	possesse 120	shreue 45	fellowe 89
Wisdome 35	downe 119	before 88	refuse 17	plaigue 53	nowe 64
Wisdome 37	growne 65	before 90	ryse 106	shreine 45	nowe 65
forme 146	nyne 2	more 5	eate 5	shreeve 44	nowe 122
spane 128	shape 92	more 45	entreate 145	gyve 127	knowe 13
tane 66	helpe 71	moore 44	maiestrate 146	gyve 146	growe 13
	are 107	moore 45	state 67	lyve 83	
captaine 114	heare 1	sore 10	grote 2	we 18	
discipline 113	heare 31	ccure 143	quyte 78	we 18	
Lincolne 1	heare 33	figure 102	pceaue 92	we 41	
Lincolne 50					

F, INITIAL

*	*	*	*	*	*
ffraunc 127	fellowe 89	fishes 86	for 76	forgyven 111	fower 3
fancies 84	fellowes 63	flanders 127	for 84	forme 146	freind 143
fayth 141	figure 102	for 9	for 98	forwarne 94	freind- 90
feed 87	find 131	for 12	for 110	foule 108	frend- 27
feet 111	first 93	for 59	forbid 96	found 147	from 66

F, MEDIAL

*	*	*	*	*	*
safer 112	aford 133	Beeff 3	before 90	offend 61	sufferd 4
Safes 43	handycraftes 71	before 88	refuse 17	thoffendor 123	ruffians 84

F, MEDIAL

*	*	*	*	*
offyc 98	infeccion 14	offend 61	oft 94	lyft 109
Shreiff 41	infect 10	offyc 98	ruff 79	plentyfull 42
lift 110	infected 12	thoffendor 123	ruffians 84	quallyfy 119
Comfort¬ 137	infected 13	loff 7	sufferd 4	

F, TERMINAL

*	*	*	*	*	*
shreef 41	sealf 85	of 19	of 62	of 99	yf 123
Beeff 3	sealf 146	of 30	of 67	of 99	yf 135
Shreiff 41	himsealf 105	of 31	of 70	of 121	yf 142
loff 7	half 7	of 32	of 71	of 124	yf 147
ruff 79	of 8	of 35	of 73	of 126	
if 91	of 12	of 37	of 79	of 131	
sealf 85	of 15	of 38	of 83	yf 4	
sealf 85	of 17	of 39	of 94	yf 95	

G, INITIAL

*	*	*	*	*	*
gainst 95	go 127	god 105	good 58	graunt 69	growe 13
gainst 105	god 88	god 106	good 59	graunt 72	growne 65
gainst 106	god 96	god 135	good 90	graunt 72	gyve 127
geat 69	god 98	god 95	gospell 88	great 5	gyve 146
gentlemen 144	god 102	good 9	gott 68	great 124	gyven 103
go 125	god 104	good 57	gott 80	grote 2	

G, MEDIAL

*	*	*	*	*	*
against 109	dogg¬ 135	straingers 20	kinge 145	king¬ 19	charge 55
against 134	portigall 128	straingers 70	Ingland 73	king¬ 26	vrging 94
aged 83	waight 7	straingers 74	Ingland 129	king¬ 77	argo 5
lugage 75	right 85	straingers 119	thing¬ 21	shilling¬ 2	forgyven 111
advauntage 71	plaigue 53	straingers 130	thing¬ 40	togeather 16	lugage 75
ymagin 74	figure 102	straingers 139	thing¬ 68	dogg¬ 135	taught 80

G, MEDIAL

*	*	*	*
thoughts 90	enough 10	brought 67	wrought 84
although 69	rough 55	through 14	

G, TERMINAL

*	*	*	*	*	*
sayeng 122	thing 69	king 122	hearing 1	eating 15	dung 12
straing 8	king 17	breaking 132	bring 8	removing 70	Dvng 13
plodding 76	king 98	doing 107	rysing 105	among 46	Charg 28
vrging 94	king 102	vndoing 8	eating 5	strong 81	

H, INITIAL

*	*	*	*	*	*
had 63	hath 73	haue 68	heare 62	him 122	how 22
had 66	hath 98	he 1	hearing 1	himsealf 105	how 28
had 80	hath 100	he 102	helpe 71	his 98	how 81
had 80	hath 102	he 123	hiddious 132	his 102	how 82
half 7	haue 13	hear 30	him 4	his 103	howe 92
hand 81	haue 18	heare 1	him 22	his 103	howe 117
hand 85	haue 37	heare 31	him 30	his 103	howses 120
hand- 108	haue 46	heare 33	him 42	his 115	howskeeper 58
handycraftes	haue 51	heare 38	him 89	hold 26	hurly 113
harber 127	haue 55	heare 41	him 100	hold 26	
harry 1	haue 64	heare 42	him 103	hold 53	
hart 9	haue 65	heare 43	him 104	horrible 92	
has 12	haue 67	heare 57	him 105	hound 122	

H, MEDIAL

*	*	*	*	*	*
Charg 28	watchins 59	right 85	inhumanyty 140	shark 86	shilling- 2
charge 55	watchins 43	taught 80	shake 14	Sher 26	worship 59
Charterd 138	choose 70	thoughts 90	shall 41	Sher 30	shoold 81
wretched 74	adheres 129	brought 67	shall 92	fishes 86	shoold 82
Chidd 73	waight 7	wrought 84	shape 92	Bushell 3	shoold 83

H, MEDIAL

*

*	*	*	*	*	*
shoold 124	that 111	the 66	their 145	another 87	what 17
shoold 127	that 117	the 67	theise 12	Brother 43	what 36
short 124	that 129	the 69	theise 67	Brother 59	what 37
showe 19	that 132	the 70	theise 144	Arther 43	what 55
shr 38.1	that 135	the 70	them 37	thinck 138	what 61
shreef 41	that 136	the 71	them 52	thing 69	what 68
shreeve 44	that¬ 88	the 71	them 53	thing¬ 21	what 80
Shreiff 41	clothd 79	the 73	them 54	thing¬ 40	what 104
Shreue 45	The 30	the 74	them 72	thing¬ 68	what 106
Shreue 45	the 8	the 88	them 111	thipp 18	what 114
shrevaltry 42	the 10	the 98	them 120	this 72	what 126
Shrewsbury 25	the 11	the 102	Them 138	this 82	what 138
Shrewsbury 30	the 12	the 109	Then 55	this 89	what¬ 9
Shrewsbury 32	the 14	the 116	then 6	this 101	when 63
Shrewsbury 38.	the 15	the 121	then 104	this 107	when 118
Shro 29	the 17	the 122	then 112	this 139	where 129
thanck 59	the 19	the 126	ther 118	this 140	wherin 65
thappostle 94	the 20	the 136	there 63	thoffendor 123	whether 125
thart 58	the 21	the 139	thers 147	those 56	whett 134
that 1	the 24	the 145	they 5	those 108	which 8
that 4	the 26	the 146	they 6	thoughts 90	which 14
that 21	the 28	their 6	they 8	aucthoryty 78	which 91
that 51	the 31	their 39	they 10	aucthoryty 94	which 94
that 56	the 32	their 53	they 13	although 69	whiles 39
that 62	the 39	their 75	they 39	throne 103	who 116
that 64	the 46	their 75	they 40	throtes 134	whose 113
that 72	the 51	their 75	they 53	throts 120	why 113
that 74	the 53	their 84	togeather 16	through 14	why 129
that 77	the 56	their 120	whether 125	thus 40	why 130
that 96	the 62	their 120	other 4	thus 139	
that 105	the 64	their 134	other 7	Arthur 59	
that 109	the 65	their 137	other 84	thy 59	

H, TERMINAL

*	*	*	*	*	*
which 8	such 63	trash 10	hath 98	both 34	ch
which 14	such 131	trash 10	hath 100	both 34	w 70
which 91	although 69	wash 108	hath 102	tooth 76	th 22
which 94	enough 10	momtanish 140	oth 10	earth 104	th
much 71	rough 55	banysh 125	both 33	earth 133	w 85
much 124	through 14	th 116	both 34	fayth 141	
such 21	sh 28	hath 73	both 34	byth 58	

I, SOLITARY

*	*	*	*	*	*
I 28	I 35	I 58	I 58	I 89	I 95

I, INITIAL

*	*	*	*	*	*
Iarman 128	in 6	in 95	incident 115	is 5	is 118
Ile 80	in 8	in 95	infeccion 14	is 8	is 123
Ingland 73	in 13	in 107	infect 10	is 13	is 139
Ingland 129	in 21	in 113	infected 12	is 62	
Iustyce 99	in 26	in 113	infected 13	is 68	
if 91	in 77	in 121	inhumanyty 14	is 112	
in 5	in 79	in 132	insolenc 81	is 113	

I, MEDIAL

*	*	*	*	*	*
maier 24	against 134	captaine 114	infeccion 14	audience 47	their 53
maiestrate 146	straing 8	certainly 97	adicion 118	plodding 76	their 75
saies 141	straingers 20	bid 100	discipline 113	hiddious 132	their 75
plaigue 53	straingers 70	forbid 96	mediation 145	discipline 113	their 75
waight 7	straingers 74	bin 66	adicion 118	Shreif 41	their 84
gainst 95	straingers 119	incident 115	did 94	freind 143	their 120
gainst 105	straingers 130	fancies 84	obedienc 94	freind 90	their 120
gainst 106	straingers 139	scilens 50	obedienc 113	their 6	their 134
against 109	straingers 4	ansportacion 76	obedienc 114	their 39	their 137

I, MEDIAL

*

their 145	him 42	this 72	Linc 35	hearing 1	prentisses 22
theise 12	him 89	this 82	Linc 41	bring 8	prentisses 23
theise 67	him 100	this 89	Linco 5	wherin 65	prentisses 23
theise 144	him 103	this 101	Lincolne 1	simplest 21	prentizes 9
Shreiue 45	him 104	this 107	Lincolne 50	sinn 93	matie 101
ruffians 84	him 105	this 139	Lincolne 53	rysing 105	removing 70
figure 102	him 122	this 140	shilling¬ 2	matie 73	¢vince 128
find 131	himsealf 105	kill 120	discipline 113	matie 121	violence 132
first 93	watchins 59	king 17	liom 121	portigall 128	will 1
fishes 86	watchins 43	king 98	slipp 122	till 65	will 4
ymagin 74	thinck 138	king 102	opynions 79	still 47	will 14
vrging 94	thing 69	king 122	montanish 140	still 116	will 19
which 8	thing¬ 21	kinge 145	doing 107	stilnes 52	will 37
which 14	thing¬ 40	king¬ 19	vndoing 8	eating 5	will 40
which 91	thing¬ 68	king¬ 26	pumpions 16	eating 15	will 53
which 94	worship 59	king¬ 77	Seriant 43	mediation 145	will 58
hiddious 132	thipp 18	breaking 132	seriant 17	¢clamation 117	will 91
Chidd 73	his 98	lift 110	seriaunt 21	nation 131	will 116
shilling¬ 2	his 102	Lin 12	appropriat 137	ynnovation 93	willd 100
whiles 39	his 103	Lin 18	horrible 92	question 21	Wisdome 35
him 4	his 103	Lin 22	watrie 9	supposytion 91	wisdome 37
him 22	his 103	Linc 8	Countrie 5	tis 10	
him 30	his 115	Linc 32	right 85	tis 93	

K, INITIAL

*

keep 28	king 17	king 122	king¬ 26	knees 110
keepes 42	king 98	kinge 145	king¬ 77	knowe 13
kill 120	king 102	king¬ 19	kneele 111	knyves 134

K, MEDIAL

*	*	*	*	*	*
speake 41	shake 14	make 112	seeke 69	lyke 86	lyke 135
speake 57	make 14	breaking 132	marke 91	lyke 109	lyke 135
speakes 41	make 111	back┐ 75	howskeeper 58	lyke 122	

K, TERMINAL

*	*	*	*
banck 39	thinck 138	look 61	mark 4
thanck 59	seek 147	shark 86	mark 89

L, SOLITARY

*	*
L 24	L 38

L, INITIAL

*	*	*	*	*	*
Leade 56	Linc 32	lawe 121	lett┐ 30	lugage 75	lyvd 63
Let 90	Linc 35	le 102	letts 141	lyft 109	lyve 83
Lett┐ 42	Linc 41	leade 121	levenpence 2	lyke 86	
Lin 12	Linco 5	lent 98	lift 110	lyke 109	
Lin 18	Lincolne 1	lent 102	liom 121	lyke 122	
Lin 22	Lincolne 50	let┐ 43	loff 7	lyke 135	
Linc 8	Lincolne 53	lets 89	look 61	lyke 135	

L, MEDIAL

*	*	*	*	*	*
alas 68	half 7	all 49	calls 104	although 69	clement 123
alas 122	all 23	all 60	portigall 128	shrevaltry 42	clothd 79
alas 122	all 34	all 73	shall 41	sealues 46	elament┐ 136
sealf 85	all 38	all 95	shall 92	horrible 92	kneele 111
sealf 85	all 38	all 96	enstalls 105	noble 30	weele 31
sealf 85	all 40	all 137	quallyfy 119	noble 144	weele 33
sealf 146	all 45	all 140	palsey 11	bloody 66	weele 38
himsealf 105	all 48	all 142	palsey 12	┌clamation 117	weele 142

L, MEDIAL

*	*	*	*	*	*
rebell 114	shilling⌐ 2	shilling⌐ 2	woold 18	pleasd 130	braule 78
rebell 118	kill 120	fellowe 89	woold 18	plentyfull 42	deule 53
rebell 119	till 65	fellowes 63	woold 64	ampler 101	deule 56
rebells 109	still 47	calls 104	woold 86	simplest 21	foule 108
fellowe 89	still 116	enstalls 105	woold 87	symple 22	youle 119
fellowes 63	will 1	rebells 109	woold 125	symple 23	youle 142
Bushell 3	will 4	quallyfy 119	woold 130	symple 23	rule 46
gospell 88	will 14	certainly 97	woold 133	discipline 113	rule 54
tell 80	will 19	only 102	woold 138	plodding 76	rule 56
tell 89	will 37	hold 26	told 95	Earle 30	rule 100
quelld 82	will 40	hold 26	violence 132	Earle 31	plentyfull 42
well 117	will 53	hold 53	insolenc 81	earle 32	sowles 106
helpe 71	will 58	coold 64	Doll 42	meerly 8	prevayle 81
flanders 127	will 91	coold 67	Doll 58	hurly 113	sylenct 78
Ingland 73	will 116	shoold 81	Doll 88	slipp 122	
Ingland 129	willd 100	shoold 82	Lincolne 1	gentlemen 144	
Ile 80	stilnes 52	shoold 83	Lincolne 50	thappostle 94	
scilens 50	quelld 82	shoold 124	Lincolne 53	ptly 14	
whiles 39	willd 100	shoold 127	plaigue 53	ruld 142	

L, TERMINAL

*	*	*	*	*
all 23	shall 41	tell 89	will 14	Doll 42
all 34	shall 92	well 117	will 19	Doll 58
all 38	rebell 114	kill 120	will 37	Doll 88
all 38	rebell 118	till 65	will 40	plentyfull 42
all 40	rebell 119	still 47	will 53	
all 45	Bushell 3	still 116	will 58	
all 48	gospell 88	will 1	will 91	
all 49	tell 80	will 4	will 116	
portigall 128				

M, INITIAL

*	*	*	*	*	*
made 42	marry 70	mayer 28	mercy 19	moor 49	more 45
made 136	marry 96	me 1	mercy 19	moor 51	much 71
maier 24	mas 58	me 3	mercy 147	moor 55	much 124
maiestrate 14	master 142	me 57	moutanish 140	moor 58	must 130
make 14	masters 27	me 90	moo 97	moor 61	mutyes 115
make 111	masters 29	mediation 145	moor 39	moor 72	my 51
make 112	masters 57	meerly 8	moor 41	moor 142	my 29
man 83	matie 73	men 35	moor 41	moor 144	my 38
mark 4	matie 101	men 37	moor 45	moore 44	my 42
mark 89	matie 121	men 67	moor 45	moore 45	my 59
marke 91	may 141	men 86	moor 46	moorne 123	mynds 108
marry 18	may 147	mercy 17	moor 49	more 5	

M, MEDIAL

*	*	*	*	*	*
(e)clamation 117	among 46	temper 131	Come 4	armes 95	Countrymen 29
element- 136	ampler 101	simplest 21	Wisdome 35	forme 146	tymes 66
name 26	Submyt 144	himsealf 105	wisdome 37	inhumanyty 140	symple 22
name 103	clement 123	Comand 47	Comfort- 137	pumpions 16	symple 23
name 115	gentlemen 144	Comaund 52	Coms 14	nvmber 51	symple 23
same 85	remoued 72	Comaund 99	moutanish 140	ymagin 74	
same 108	removing 70	yeoman 43	Iarman 128	Countrymen 27	

M, TERMINAL

*	*	*	*	*	*
them 37	them 72	him 4	him 89	him 105	from 66
them 52	them 111	him 22	him 100	him 122	
them 53	them 120	him 30	him 103	com 124	
them 54	them 136	him 42	him 104	liom 121	

N, SOLITARY

*

n 115

N, INITIAL

*	*	*	?	*	*
name 26	nay 129	no 38	nor 136	not 83	nowe 64
name 103	need¬ 130	no 95	not 1	not 102	nowe 65
name 115	no 18	no 118	not 18	not 129	nowe 122
nation 131	no 19	no 147	not 37	not 133	noyce 72
nature 126	no 38	noble 30	not 38	not 136	nvmber 51
nay 12	no 38	noble 144	not 53	not 136	nyne 2
nay 89	no 38	nobles 3	not 62	not 137	
nay 97	no 38	nor 136	not 67	now 22	

N, MEDIAL

*		*	*	*	*
banck 39	and 82	Ingland 73	banysh 125	levenpence 2	present 62
fancies 84	and 85	Ingland 129	inhumanyty 140	enstalls 105	incident 115
thanck 59	and 86	Comand 47	obedienc 94	scilens 50	thinck 138
and 3	and 95	stand 142	obedienc 113	Enter 24	Linc 8
and 10	and 99	spane 128	obedienc 114	entreate 145	Linc 32
and 13	and 100	tane 66	audience 47	incident 115	Linc 35
and 16	and 101	momtanish 140	violence 132	gentlemen 144	Linc 41
and 42	and 108	Cannot 54	insolenc 81	lent 98	Linco 5
and 51	and 110	Cannot 56	sylenct 78	lent 102	Lincolne 1
and 55	and 121	cannot 70	levenpence 2	plentyfull 42	Lincolne 50
and 58	and 135	cannot 114	obedyenc 39	elament¬ 136	Lincolne 53
and 66	and 140	another 87	offend 61	clement 123	prvince 128
and 72	and 147	ruffians 84	thoffendor 123	vnreuerent 110	freind 143
and 75	hand 81	transportacion 7	frend¬ 27	prentisses 22	freind¬ 90
and 76	hand 85	Seriant 43	sayeng 122	prentisses 23	find 131
and 77	hand¬ 108	seriant 17	penny 7	prentisses 23	captaine 114
handycraftes 71		any 128	enough 10	prentizes 9	discipline 113
flanders 127		any 129	ravenous 66	prenty 22	infeccion 14

<u>N</u>, MEDIAL

*	*	*	*	*	*
infect 10	king 17	certainly 97	Cannot 56	Comaund 52	Dvng 13
infected 12	king 98	sinn 93	cannot 70	Comaund 99	vnreuerent 110
infected 13	king 102	insolenc 81	cannot 114	found 147	vnto 138
Ingland 73	king 122	gainst 95	ynnovation 93	hound 122	owne 6
Ingland 129	kinge 145	gainst 105	penny 7	sound 89	owne 103
straing 8	king¬ 19	gainst 106	throne 103	sounde 117	downe 22
straingers 20	king¬ 26	against 109	among 46	dung 12	downe 40
straingers 70	king¬ 77	against 134	strong 81	seriaunt 21	downe 73
straingers 74	breaking 132	watchins 59	only 102	graunt 69	downe 119
straingers 119	shilling¬ 2	watchins 43	opynions 79	graunt 72	growne 65
straingers 130	doing 107	kneele 111	pumpions 16	graunt 72	mynds 108
straingers 139	vndoing 8	knees 110	reasons 85	advauntage 71	nyne 2
strainge<u>rs</u> 4	hearing 1	knowe 13	forwarne 94	Countrey 6	opynions 79
plodding 76	bring 8	knyves 134	patterne 82	Countrie 5	ynnovation 93
vrging 94	rysing 105	stilnes 52	moorne 123	Country 5	
thing¬ 69	eating 5	Lincolne 1	spurne 135	Country 126	
thing¬ 21	eating 15	Lincolne 50	psnyp 9	Countrymen 27	
thing¬ 40	removing 70	Lincolne 53	psnyps 15	Countrymen 29	
thing¬ 68	inhumanyty 140	Cannot 54	ffraunc 127	vndoing 8	

<u>N</u>, TERMINAL

*	*	*	*	*	*
an 83	then 112	even 46	in 95	Lin 22	pdon 143
an 133	when 63	gyven 103	in 95	wherin 65	sportacion 76
can 112	when 118	forgyven 111	in 107	sinn 93	infeccion 14
can 116	men 35	in 5	in 113	on 53	adicion 118
can 117	men 37	in 6	in 113	on 83	mediation 145
man 83	men 67	in 8	in 121	on 86	pclamation 117
yeoman 43	men 86	in 13	in 132	on 87	nation 131
Iarman 128	gentlemen 144	in 21	bin 66	on 87	ynnovation 93
Then 55	Countrymen 27	in 26	ymagin 74	on 91	question 21
then 6	Countrymen 29	in 77	Lin 12	on 104	vpposytion 91
then 104	euen 113	in 79	Lin 18	on 133	doon 141

61

N, TERMINAL
```
*
vppon 18
```

O, SOLITARY
```
*                    *
o 107                o 16
```

O, INITIAL
```
*            *            *            *            *
obay 100     of 19        offend 61    only 102     other 84
obay 116     of 30        offyc 98     opynions 79  our 5
obay 146     of 31        oft 94       or 35        our 6
obedienc 94  of 32        on 53        or 117       our 13
obedienc 113 of 35        on 83        or 127       our 142
obedienc 114 of 37        on 86        or 128       our 143
obedyenc 39  of 38        on 87        orderd 82    out 132
of 8         of 39        on 87        ore 39       owed 136
of 12        of 62        on 91        oth 10       owne 6
of 15        of 67        on 104       other 4      owne 103
of 17        of 70        on 133       other 7
```

O, MEDIAL
```
*            *             *             *              *             *
abode 133    Comaund 52    Country 126   pdon 143       for 12        before 90
both 33      Comaund 99    Countrymen 27 doon 141       for 59        Comfort⌐ 137
both 34      Come 4        Countrymen 29 thoffendor 123 for 76        foule 108
both 34      Comfort⌐ 137  dogg⌐ 135     doubt 147      for 84        found 147
both 34      Coms 14       doing 107     downe 22       for 98        fower 3
both 34      coold 64      vndoing 8     downe 40       for 110       god 88
Lincolne 1   coold 67      Doll 42       downe 73       forbid 96     god 96
Lincolne 50  cost⌐ 76      Doll 58       downe 119      forgyven 111  god 98
Lincolne 53  Countrey 6    Doll 88       yeoman 43      forme 146     god 102
com 124      Countrie 5    Wisdome 35    aford 133      forwarne 94   god 104
Comand 47    Country 5     wisdome 37    for 9          before 88     god 105
```

O, MEDIAL

*	*	*	*	*	*
god 106	how 82	moor 45	not 129	shoold 127	poor 75
god 135	howe 92	moor 45	not 133	woold 18	choose 70
good 9	howe 117	moor 46	not 136	woold 18	rootes 8
good 57	howses 120	moor 49	not 136	woold 64	tooth 76
good 58	howskeeper 58	moor 49	not 137	woold 86	vppon 18
good 59	showe 19	moor 51	another 87	woold 87	poor 8
good 90	violence 132	moor 55	Cannot 54	woold 125	poor 68
gospell 86	liom 121	moor 58	Cannot 56	woold 130	poor 71
gott 68	nsportacion 76	moor 61	cannot 70	woold 133	poor 75
gott 80	infeccion 14	moor 72	cannot 114	woold 136	portigall 128
thoffendor 123	adicion 118	moor 142	enough 10	doon 141	port~ 76
hold 26	opynions 79	moor 144	ravenous 86	aford 133	transportacion 76
hold 26	pumpions 16	moore 44	ynnovation 93	moor 39	possesse 120
hold 53	mediation 145	moore 45	now 22	moor 41	thappostle 94
choose 70	proclamation 117	moorne 123	nowe 64	moor 41	supposytion 91
shoold 81	nation 131	more 5	nowe 65	moor 45	pounde 2
shoold 82	ynnovation 93	more 45	nowe 122	moor 45	power 99
shoold 83	question 21	renoued 72	knowe 13	moor 46	from 66
shoold 124	supposytion 91	removing 70	noyce 72	moor 49	throne 103
shoold 127	hiddious 132	noble 30	good 9	moor 49	strong 81
horrible 92	plodding 76	noble 144	good 57	moor 51	rootes 8
short 124	loff 7	nobles 3	good 58	moor 55	appropriat 137
aucthoryty 78	look 61	nor 136	good 59	moor 58	error 95
aucthoryty 94	bloody 66	nor 136	good 90	moor 61	error 126
those 56	clothd 79	not 1	bloody 66	moor 72	Brother 43
those 108	fellowe 89	not 18	stood 21	moor 142	Brother 59
whose 113	fellowes 63	not 37	look 61	moor 144	grote 2
hound 122	momtanish 140	not 38	coold 64	moore 44	throtes 134
thoughts 90	among 46	not 53	coold 67	moore 45	throts 120
although 69	moo 97	not 62	shoold 81	moorne 123	rough 55
how 22	moor 39	not 67	shoold 82	poor 8	rout 116
how 28	moor 41	not 83	shoold 83	poor 68	barbarous 131
how 61	moor 41	not 102	shoold 124	poor 71	brought 67

63

O, MEDIAL

*	*	*	*ᵘ	*ᵘ	*ᵘ
through 14	voyce 51	yoʳ 113	Yoᵘ 51	yoᵘ 66	yoᵘ 100
wrought 84	woold 18	yoʳ 126	yoᵘ 17	yoᵘ 67	yoᵘ 104
growe 13	woold 18	yoʳ 134	yoᵘ 17	yoᵘ 68	yoᵘ 106
growne 65	woold 64	yoʳ 137	yoᵘ 18	yoᵘ 69	yoᵘ 109
troy 7	woold 86	yoʳ 146	yoᵘ 18	yoᵘ 69	yoᵘ 112
insolenc 81	woold 87	ryot 113	yoᵘ 21	yoᵘ 74	yoᵘ 125
reasons 85	woold 125	ryotous 55	yoᵘ 22	yoᵘ 77	yoᵘ 125
sore 10	woold 130	you 13	yoᵘ 28	yoᵘ 79	yoᵘ 127
sorry 9	woold 133	you 107	yoᵘ 35	yoᵘ 80	yoᵘ 129
sound 89	woold 138	you 127	yoᵘ 36	yoᵘ 80	yoᵘ 130
sounde 117	worship 59	youle 119	yoᵘ 37	yoᵘ 80	yoᵘ 130
sowles 106	sword 103	youle 142	yoᵘ 46	yoᵘ 83	yoᵘ 133
togeather 16	yoʳ 46	your 77	yoᵘ 55	yoᵘ 86	yoᵘ 135
told 95	yoʳ 72	your 93	yoᵘ 61	yoᵘ 89	yoᵘ 136
tooth 76	yoʳ 78	your 108	yoᵘ 61	yoᵘ 91	yoᵘ 138
stood 21	yoʳ 79	your 110	yoᵘ 62	yoᵘ 92	yoᵘ 142
topt 64	yoʳ 90	your 111	yoᵘ 63	yoᵘ 95	yoᵘ 144
traytor 116	yoʳ 106	your 124	yoᵘ 64	yoᵘ 95	yoᵘ 147
ryotous 55	yoʳ 113	your 140	yoᵘ 65	yoᵘ 97	

O, TERMINAL

*	*	*	*	*	*
Linco 5	who 116	moo 97	to 56	to 119	to 143
do 6	no 18	Shro 29	to 67	to 122	to 144
do 17	no 19	so 124	to 94	to 124	to 145
do 18	no 38	so 147	to 98	to 125	to 146
do 61	no 38	to 3	to 100	to 127	vnto 138
do 104	no 38	to 4	to 101	to 128	yo 79
do 106	no 38	to 8	to 101	to 128	
do 141	no 38	to 9	to 106	to 129	
go 125	no 95	to 10	to 111	to 131	
go 127	no 118	to 17	to 111	to 137	
argo 5	no 147	to 52	to 113	to 139	

P, INITIAL

*

Peace 1	peace 28	peace 62	plentyfull 42	possesse 120	present 62
Peace 35	peace 35	peace 64	plodding 76	pounde 2	prevayle 81
palsey 11	peace 50	peace 65	poor 8	power 99	pumpions 16
palsey 12	peace 50	peace 109	poor 68	prentisses 22	put 119
passe 4	peace 50	peace 110	poor 71	prentisses 23	
patterne 82	peace 53	penny 7	poor 75	prentisses 23	
peace 28	peace 60	plaigue 53	portigall 128	prentizes 9	
peace 28	peace 60	pleasd 130	port¬ 76	prenty 22	

P, MEDIAL

*

shape 92	discipline 113	simplest 21	opynions 79	spane 128	transportacion 76
appropriat 137	thipp 18	symple 22	thappostle 94	trespas 124	spurne 135
thappostle 94	slipp 122	symple 23	supposytion 91	speake 41	supposytion 91
captaine 114	helpe 71	symple 23	vppon 18	speake 57	vppõ 19
keepes 42	temper 131	levenpence 2	vppõ 19	speakes 41	vppõ 61
howskeeper 58	pumpions 16	appropriat 137	vppõ 61	desperat 107	vppon 18
accept 19	ampler 101	topt 64	appropriat 137	gospell 88	psnyps 15

P, TERMINAL

*

keep 28	thipp 18	vp 65	vp 110	psnyp 9
worship 59	slipp 122	vp 90	vp 146	

Q, INITIAL

*

quallyfy 119	quelld 82	question 21	quyte 78

R, INITIAL

*

ravenous 86	rebell 118	refuse 17	right 85	rout 116	ruld 142
reasons 85	rebell 119	removed 72	rootes 8	ruff 79	rule 46
rebell 114	rebells 109	removing 70	rough 55	ruffians 84	rule 54

<u>R</u>, INITIAL

*	*	*	*	*	*
rule 56	rule 100	ryot 113	ryotous 55	ryse 106	rysing 105

<u>R</u>, MEDIAL

*	*	*	*	*	*
barbarous 131	marry 18	sufferd 4	certainly 97	first 93	prentisses 23
harber 127	marry 70	Charterd 138	ffraunc 127	vnreuerent 110	prentisses 23
are 107	marry 96	basterd 12	freind 143	forbid 96	prentizes 9
heare 1	warrs 112	bere 40	freind 90	orderd 82	prenty 22
heare 31	warrs 113	beres 93	frend 27	afoord 133	present 62
heare 33	Arther 43	adheres 129	from 66	sword 103	prevayle 81
heare 38	Arthur 59	there 63	graunt 69	ore 39	appropriat 137
heare 41	earth 104	where 129	graunt 72	before 88	appropriat 137
heare 42	earth 133	vnreuerent 110	graunt 72	before 90	Surrey 24
heare 43	hart 9	twere 95	great 5	more 5	Surrey 27
heare 57	Charterd 138	wherin 65	great 124	more 45	Surrey 31
heare 62	thart 58	Seriant 43	grote 2	moore 44	Surrey 38
teares 108	braule 78	seriant 17	growe 13	moore 45	<u>S</u>urrey 48
argo 5	breaking 132	seriaunt 21	growne 65	sore 10	horrible 92
Charg 28	breed 10	meerly 8	shreef 41	forgyven 111	error 95
charge 55	bring 8	patterne 82	shreeve 44	forme 146	error 126
hearing 1	Brother 43	error 95	Shreiff 41	moorne 123	warrs 112
shark 86	Brother 59	error 126	Shreiue 45	horrible 92	warrs 113
mark 4	brought 67	flanders 127	Shreue 45	sorry 9	harry 1
mark 89	handycraftes 71	straingers 20	shrevalty 42	worship 59	marry 18
marke 91	Credyt 51	straingers 70	Shrewsbury 25	Comfort 137	marry 70
Earle 30	Cry 61	straingers 74	Shrewsbury 30	short 124	marry 96
Earle 31	dread 99	straingers 119	Shrewsbury 32	portigall 128	sorry 9
earle 32	desperat 107	straingers 130	Shrewsbury 38,1	port 76	transportacion
armes 95	mercy 17	straingers 139	Shro 29	transportacion 76	trash 10
Iarman 128	mercy 19	thers 147	throne 103	forwarne 94	trash 10
forwarne 94	mercy 19	masters 27	throtes 134	aucthoryty 78	traytor 116
barbarous 131	mercy 147	masters 29	throts 120	aucthoryty 94	straing 8
harry 1	orderd 82	masters 57	through 14	prentisses 22	straingers 20

66

R, MEDIAL

*	*	*	*	*	*
straingers 70	trespas 124	Countrie 5	Countrymen 29	Surrey 24	shrewsbury 32
straingers 74	trewe 16	troy 7	(cure 143	Surrey 27	Shrewsbury 38.1
straingers 119	trewe 88	strong 81	figure 102	Surrey 31	Sury 48
straingers 130	trewe 141	shrevaltry 42	nature 126	Surrey 38	vrging 94
straingers 139	enteate 145	Country 5	hurly 113	Surrey 48	wretched 74
straingers 4	Country 6	Country 126	spurne 135	Shrewsbury 25	wrought 84
maiestrate 146	wattie 9	Countrymen 27	Surr 37	Shrewsbury 30	desyres 77

R, TERMINAL

*	*	*	*	*	*
ar 21	other 84	shr 38.1	for 12	moor 61	your 93
ar 35	another 87	their 6	for 59	moor 72	your 108
ar 35	Brother 43	their 39	for 76	moor 142	your 110
ar 36	Brother 59	their 53	for 84	moor 144	your 111
ar 39	Arther 43	their 75	for 98	poor 8	your 124
ar 97	maier 24	their 75	for 110	poor 68	your 140
ar 107	ampler 101	their 75	nor 136	poor 71	yor 46
ar 115	howskeeper 58	their 84	nor 136	poor 75	yor 72
hear 30	temper 131	their 120	moor 39	error 95	yor 78
nvmber 51	Enter 24	their 120	moor 41	error 126	yor 79
harber 127	master 142	their 134	moor 41	traytor 116	yor 90
safer 112	butter 2	their 137	moor 45	Surr 37	yor 106
Sher 26	euer 112	their 145	moor 45	Arthur 59	yor 113
Sher 30	wer 63	or 35	moor 46	our 5	yor 113
ther 118	wer 95	or 117	moor 49	our 6	yor 126
togeather 16	wer 137	or 127	moor 49	our 13	yor 134
whether 125	fower 3	or 128	moor 51	our 142	yor 137
other 4	power 99	thoffendor 123	moor 55	our 143	yor 146
other 7	mayer 28	for 9	moor 58	your 77	

S, INITIAL

*	*	*	*	*	*
Safes 43	Surrey 38	see 1	shoold 124	sowles 106	straingers 13
Seriant 43	Sury 48	see 74	shoold 127	spane 128	straingers 13
Sher 26	safer 112	seek 147	short 124	speake 41	straingers 4
Sher 30	saies 141	seeke 69	showe 19	speake 57	strong 81
Shreiff 41	same 85	seriant 17	shr 38 1	speakes 41	such 21
Shreiue 45	same 108	seriaunt 21	shreef 41	spurne 135	such 63
Shreue 45	say 17	sett 90	shreeve 44	stand 142	such 131
Shrewsbury 25	say 22	sh 28	shrevaltry 42	state 67	supposition 9
Shrewsbury 30	say 35	shake 14	simplest 21	still 47	sword 103
Shrewsbury 32	say 122	shall 41	sinn 93	still 116	sylenct 78
Shrewsbury 38	sayeng 122	shall 92	slipp 122	stilnes 52	symple 22
Shro 29	scilens 50	shape 92	so 124	stood 21	symple 23
Submyt 144	sealf 85	shark 86	so 147	straing 8	symple 23
Surr 37	sealf 85	shilling¬ 2	sore 10	straingers 20	sytt 77
Surrey 24	sealf 146	shoold 81	sorry 9	straingers 70	
Surrey 27	sealues 46	shoold 82	sound 89	straingers 74	
Surrey 31		shoold 83	sounde 117	straingers 11	

S, MEDIAL

*	*	*	*	*	*
pleasd 130	desperat 107	theise 144	gainst 105	psnyp 9	must 130
case 139	trespas 124	fishes 86	gainst 106	psnyps 15	vsd 139
trash 10	possesse 120	momtanish 140	against 109	worship 59	Shrewsbury 25
trash 10	maiestrate 146	prentisses 22	against 134	first 93	Shrewsbury 30
wash 108	simplest 21	prentisses 23	those 56	passe 4	Shrewsbury 32
reasons 85	detested 134	prentisses 23	those 108	possesse 120	Shrewsbury 38.1
passe 4	question 21	palsey 11	whose 113	prentisses 22	howses 120
basterd¬ 12	desyres 77	palsey 12	chose 70	prentisses 23	howskeeper 58
master 142	discipline 113	himsealf 105	gospell 88	prentisses 23	ryse 106
masters 27	wisdome 35	insolenc 81	possesse 120	possesse 120	banysh 125
masters 29	wisdome 37	transportacion 76	cost¬ 76	refuse 17	rysing 105
masters 57	theise 12	enstalls 105	thappostle 94	Bushell 3	
present 62	theise 67	gainst 95	supposytion 91	Iustyce 99	

68

S, TERMINAL

*	*	*	*	*	*
as 13	babes 63	prentisses 23	is 118	enstalls 105	masters 29
as 64	knees 110	howses 120	is 123	rebells 109	masters 57
as 77	Safes 43	ndycraftes 71	is 139	Coms 14	warrs 112
as 84	fishes 86	rootes 8	his 98	ruffians 84	warrs 113
as 88	saies 141	throtes 134	his 102	scilens 50	lets 89
as 88	fancies 84	sealues 46	his 103	watchins 59	thoughts 90
as 107	speakes 41	knyves 134	his 103	opynions 79	throts 120
as 115	whiles 39	fellowes 63	his 103	pumpions 16	letts 141
as 123	fellowes 63	babyes 75	his 115	reasons 85	thus 40
as 125	sowles 106	eyes 10	this 72	psnyps 15	thus 139
as 135	armes 95	mutyes 115	this 82	flanders 127	hiddious 132
as 141	tymes 66	prentizes 9	this 89	straingers 20	ravenous 86
has 12	stilnes 52	is 5	this 101	straingers 70	barbarous 131
alas 68	keepes 42	is 8	this 107	straingers 74	ryotous 55
alas 122	teares 108	is 13	this 139	straingers 119	vs 13
alas 122	beres 93	is 62	this 140	straingers 130	vs 94
mas 58	adheres 129	is 68	tis 10	straingers 139	vs 141
trespas 124	desyres 77	is 112	tis 93	thers 147	
mynds 108	prentisses 22	is 113	calls 104	masters 27	
	prentisses 23				

T, INITIAL

*	*	*	*	*	*
The 30	thart 58	that 96	the 10	the 28	the 66
Then 55	that 1	that 105	the 11	the 31	the 67
tane 66	that 4	that 109	the 12	the 32	the 69
taught 80	that 21	that 111	the 14	the 39	the 70
teares 108	that 51	that 117	the 15	the 46	the 70
tell 80	that 56	that 129	the 17	the 51	the 71
tell 89	that 62	that 132	the 19	the 53	the 71
temper 131	that 64	that 135	the 20	the 56	the 73
th 116	that 72	that 136	the 21	the 62	the 74
thanck 59	that 74	that, 88	the 24	the 64	the 88
thappostle 94	that 77	the 8	the 26	the 65	the 98

T, INITIAL

*

*	*	*	*	*	*
the 102	their 137	they 8	those 108	to 94	to 144
the 109	their 145	they 10	thoughts 90	to 98	to 145
the 116	theise 12	they 13	throne 103	to 100	to 146
the 121	theise 67	they 39	throtes 134	to 101	togeather 16
the 122	theise 144	they 40	throts 120	to 101	told 95
the 126	them 37	they 53	through 14	to 106	tooth 76
the 136	them 52	thinck 138	thus 40	to 111	topt 64
the 139	them 53	thing 69	thus 139	to 111	transportacio
the 145	them 54	thing¬ 21	thy 59	to 113	trash 10
the 146	them 72	thing¬ 40	till 65	to 119	trash 10
the 17	them 111	thing¬ 68	tis 10	to 122	traytor 116
their 6	them 120	thipp 18	tis 93	to 124	trespas 124
their 39	them 138	this 72	to 3	to 125	trewe 16
their 53	then 6	this 82	to 4	to 127	trewe 88
their 75	then 104	this 89	to 8	to 128	trewe 141
their 75	then 112	this 101	to 9	to 128	troy 7
their 75	ther 118	this 107	to 10	to 129	twere 95
their 84	there 63	this 139	to 17	to 131	tymes 66
their 120	thers 147	this 140	to 52	to 137	
their 120	they 5	thoffendor 12	to 56	to 139	
their 134	they 6	those 56	to 67	to 143	

T, MEDIAL

*

*	*	*	*	*	*
watchins 59	hath 100	ynnovation 93	aucthoryty 94	bett¬ 33	although 69
watchins 43	hath 102	watrie 9	wretched 74	bett¬ 50	shrevaltry 42
eate 5	eating 5	that¬ 88	detested 134	whett 134	momtanish 140
entreate 145	eating 15	what¬ 9	whether 125	Lett¬ 42	advauntage 71
maiestrate 146	mediation 145	patterne 82	let¬ 43	lett¬ 30	Enter 24
state 67	matie 73	nature 126	lets 89	letts 141	prentisses 22
togeather 16	matie 121	infected 12	Bett 70	sett 90	prentisses 23
hath 73	€clamation 117	infected 13	Bett¬ 89	handycraftes 71	prentisses 23
hath 98	nation 131	aucthoryty 78	bett¬ 31	thoughts 90	prentizes 9

T, MEDIAL

*	*	*	*	*	*
gentlemen 144	other 7	ptly 14	masters 29	strong 81	cutt 120
vnto 138	other 84	certainly 97	masters 57	maiestrate 146	mutyes 115
entreate 145	both 33	transportacion 76	detested 134	cost¬ 76	quyte 78
Countrey 6	both 34	Charterd 138	still 47	Iustyce 99	fayth 141
Countrie 5	both 34	Arther 43	still 116	patterne 82	byth 58
Country 5	both 34	Arthur 59	stilnes 52	butter 2	supposytion 91
Country 126	both 34	earth 104	question 21	Bett¬ 89	traytor 116
Countrymen 27	clothd 79	earth 133	thappostle 94	bett¬ 31	Cytty 11
Countrymen 29	another 87	portigall 128	stood 21	bett¬ 33	Cytty 14
element¬ 136	tooth 76	Comfort¬ 137	straing 8	bett¬ 50	Cytty 71
plentyfull 42	Brother 43	port¬ 76	straingers 20	Lett¬ 42	sytt 77
prenty 22	Brother 59	stand 142	straingers 70	lett¬ 30	inhumanyty 140
rootes 8	ryotous 55	state 67	straingers 74	letts 141	aucthoryty 78
grote 2	throts 120	enstalls 105	straingers 119	Cytty 11	th 22
throtes 134	gott 68	basterd¬ 12	straingers 130	Cytty 14	w 85
oth 10	gott 80	master 142	straingers 139	Cytty 71	
other 4	captaine 114	masters 27	straingers 4	butter 2	

T, TERMINAL

*	*	*	*	*	*
at 1	that 64	what 17	desperat 107	wrought 84	not 1
at 2	that 72	what 36	doubt 147	seriant 43	not 18
at 3	that 74	what 37	infect 10	seriant 17	not 37
at 75	that 77	what 55	sylenct 78	incident 115	not 38
geat 69	that 96	what 61	feet 111	lent 98	not 53
great 5	that 105	what 68	Let 90	lent 102	not 62
great 124	that 109	what 80	lift 110	clement 123	not 67
that 1	that 111	what 104	oft 94	vnreuerent 110	not 83
that 4	that 117	what 106	lyft 109	present 62	not 102
that 21	that 129	what 114	waight 7	seriaunt 21	not 129
that 51	that 132	what 126	right 85	graunt 69	not 133
that 56	that 135	what 138	taught 80	graunt 72	not 136
that 62	that 136	appropriat 137	brought 67	graunt 72	not 136

71

T, TERMINAL

*	*	*	*	*	*
not 137	thart 58	must 130	But 37	but 138	yt 17
Cannot 54	short 124	lyst 3	but 19	but 147	yt 68
Cannot 56	simplest 21	Bett 70	but 37	out 132	Credyt 51
cannot 70	gainst 95	whett 134	but 70	rout 116	Submyt 144
cannot 114	gainst 105	sett 90	but 103	put 119	w 11
ryot 113	gainst 106	gott 68	but 106	yt 4	w 12
accept 19	against 109	gott 80	but 114	yt 12	w 51
topt 64	against 134	cutt 120	but 118	yt 12	w 75
hart 9	first 93	sytt 77	but 125	yt 13	w 108

U, MEDIAL

*	*	*	*	*	*
aucthoryty 78	graunt 72	cutt 120	lugage 75	Countrymen 27	barbarous 131
aucthoryty 94	graunt 72	dung 12	much 71	Countrymen 29	ryotous 55
audience 47	advauntage 71	euen 113	much 124	found 147	out 132
pceaue 92	Shrewsbury 25	euer 112	must 130	hound 122	rout 116
haue 13	Shrewsbury 30	Shreue 45	mutyes 115	pounde 2	pumpions 16
haue 18	Shrewsbury 32	vnreuerent 110	doubt 147	sound 89	spurne 135
haue 37	Shrewsbury 38.1	eua 21	remoued 72	sounde 117	put 119
haue 46	Bushell 3	deule 53	thoughts 90	our 5	quallyfy 119
haue 51	But 37	deule 56	although 69	our 6	quelld 82
haue 55	but 19	plentyfull 42	enough 10	our 13	question 21
haue 64	but 37	refuse 17	rough 55	our 142	quyte 78
haue 65	but 70	plaigue 53	brought 67	our 143	ruff 79
haue 67	but 103	figure 102	through 14	your 77	ruffians 84
haue 68	but 106	inhumanyty 140	wrought 84	your 93	ruld 142
taught 80	but 114	hurly 113	foule 108	your 108	rule 46
braule 78	but 118	Arthur 59	youle 119	your 110	rule 54
seriaunt 21	but 125	thus 40	youle 142	your 111	rule 56
Comaund 52	but 138	thus 139	Countrey 6	your 124	rule 100
Comaund 99	but 147	Shreiue 45	Countrie 5	your 140	Submyt 144
ffraunc 127	butter 2	Iustyce 99	Country 5	hiddious 132	such 21
graunt 69	Ccure 143	sealues 46	Country 126	ravenous 86	such 63

72

U, MEDIAL

*

such 131
supposytion 91

*	* Surr 37	* Surrey 27	* Surrey 38	* Surry 48	*
	Surrey 24	Surrey 31	Surrey 48	nature 126	

U, TERMINAL

*	*	*	*	*	*
you 13	you 28	you 64	you 80	you 97	you 130
you 107	you 35	you 65	you 80	you 100	you 130
you 127	you 36	you 66	you 80	you 104	you 133
you 51	you 37	you 67	you 83	you 106	you 135
you 17	you 46	you 68	you 86	you 109	you 136
you 17	you 55	you 69	you 89	you 112	you 138
you 18	you 61	you 69	you 91	you 125	you 142
you 55	you 61	you 74	you 92	you 125	you 144
you 61	you 62	you 77	you 95	you 127	you 147
you 61	yo 63	yo 79	yo 95	yo 129	
you 18					
you 21					
yo 22					

V, INITIAL

*	*	*	*	*	*
violence 132	vnto 138	vp 90	vppõ 19	vrging 94	vs 141
vndoing 8	voyce 51	vp 110	vppõ 61	vs 13	vsd 139
vnreuerent 11	vp 65	vp 146	vppon 18	vs 94	

V, MEDIAL

*	*	*	*	*	*
ravenous 86	shrevalry 42	levenpence 2	removing 70	gyve 127	forgyven 111
advauntage 71	prevayle 81	nvmber 51	Qvince 128	gyve 146	lyve 83
Dvng 13	shreeve 44	ynnovation 93	lyvd 63	gyven 103	knyves 134

V, TERMINAL

*

mv 51

W, INITIAL

*	*	*	*	*	*
Wisdome 35	we 141	what 61	whett 134	will 19	woold 125
waight 7	wee 19	what 68	which 8	will 37	woold 130
warrs 112	weele 31	what 80	which 14	will 40	woold 133
warrs 113	weele 33	what 104	which 91	will 53	woold 138
wash 108	weele 38	what 106	which 94	will 58	worship 59
watchins 59	weele 142	what 114	whiles 39	will 91	wretched 74
watching 43	well 117	what 126	who 116	will 116	wrought 84
wattie 9	wer 63	what 138	whose 113	willd 100	t 11
W ch 70	wer 95	what- 9	why 113	wisdome 37	t 12
we 16	wer 137	when 63	why 129	woold 18	t 51
we 18	what 17	when 118	why 130	woold 18	t 75
we 41	what 36	where 129	will 1	woold 64	t 108
we 58	what 37	wherin 65	will 4	woold 86	th 22
we 69	what 55	whether 125	will 14	woold 87	th 85

W, MEDIAL

*	*	*	*	*	*
lawe 121	Shrewsbury 32	showe 19	knowe 13	downe 22	howskeeper 58
trewe 16	Shrewsbury 38.1	fellowe 89	power 99	downe 40	forwarne 94
trewe 88	owed 136	fellowes 63	growe 13	downe 73	sword 103
trewe 141	fower 3	nowe 64	sowles 106	downe 119	twere 95
Shrewsbury 25	howe 92	nowe 65	owne 6	growne 65	
Shrewsbury 30	howe 117	nowe 122	owne 103	howses 120	

W, TERMINAL

*	*	*	*	*
how 22	how 28	how 81	how 82	now 22

Y, SOLITARY

*
y 72

Y, INITIAL

*
Yo^u 51	yor 106
yeoman 43	yor 113
yf 4	yor 113
yf 95	yor 126
yf 123	yor 134
yf 135	yor 137
yf 142	yor 146
yf 147	you 13
ymagin 74	you 17
ynnovation 93	you 17
yo^u 79	you 18
yor 46	you 18
yor 72	you^u 21
yor 78	you 22
yor 79	yor 28
yo 90	yo 35

*
you^u 36	yo^u 77	you 107	yo^u 147
you 37	you 79	yo^u 109	youle 119
you 46	you 80	yo^u 112	youle 142
you 55	you 80	you 125	your 77
you 61	you 83	yo^u 125	your 93
you 61	you 86	you 127	your 108
you 62	you 89	yo^u 127	your 110
you 63	you 91	you 129	your 111
you 64	you 92	you 130	your 124
you 65	you 95	you 130	your 140
you 66	you 95	you 133	yt 4
you 67	you 97	you 135	yt 12
you 68	you 100	you 136	yt 12
you 69	yo^u 104	you 138	yt 13
you^u 69	yo 106	you 142	yt 17
yo 74		yo 144	yt 68

Y, MEDIAL

*
mayer 28	handycraftes 71	quallyfy 119	nyne 2	Countrymen 29	symple 23
sayeng 122	obedyenc 39	lyke 86	psnyp 9	ryot 113	desyres 77
prevayle 81	Credyt 51	lyke 109	psnyps 15	ryotous 55	sytt 77
fayth 141	eyes 10	lyke 122	banysh 125	ryse 106	supposytion 91
traytor 116	offyc 98	lyke 135	inhumanyty 140	rysing 105	Iustyce 99
babyes 75	gyve 127	lyke 135	knyves 134	auchoryty 78	mutyes 115
byth 58	gyve 146	lyvd 63	noyce 72	auchoryty 94	plentyfull 42
Cytty 11	gyvven 103	lyve 83	voyce 51	sylenct 78	tymes 66
Cytty 14	forgyven 111	mynds 108	opynions 79	symple 22	quyte 78
Cytty 71	lyft 109	Submyt 144	Countrymen 27	symple 23	

Y, TERMINAL

*					
obay 100	by 7	they 5	palsey 11	my 42	Country 126
obay 116	by 46	they 6	palsey 12	my 59	Shrewsbury 25
obay 146	by 78	they 8	quallyfy 119	any 128	Shrewsbury 30
day 7	by 82	they 10	thy 59	any 129	Shrewsbury 32
may 141	by 114	they 13	why 113	penny 7	Shrewsbury 38,1
may 147	by 115	they 39	why 129	troy 7	Sury 48
nay 12	by 126	they 40	why 130	Cry 61	prenty 22
nay 89	by 141	they 53	certainly 97	harry 1	Cytty 11
nay 97	by 142	surrey 24	only 102	marry 18	Cytty 14
nay 129	mercy 17	surrey 27	meerly 8	marry 70	Cytty 71
say 17	mercy 19	surrey 31	hurly 113	marry 96	inhumanyty 140
say 22	mercy 19	surrey 38	ptly 14	sorry 9	aucthoryty 78
say 35	mercy 147	Surrey 48	my 29	shrevaltry 42	
say 122	bloody 66	Countrey 6	my 38	Country 5	

Z, MEDIAL

*

prentizes 9

76

III. THE MODERN-SPELLING TEXTS

By modernizing spelling and punctuation (much of the latter as well as most of the capitalization is supplied), expanding abbreviations, normalizing speech-prefixes, and making minor alterations as noted, I have tried to make all three texts following more immediately and continuously intelligible as dramatic dialogue than they would be in type-facsimile (though "theatrical" editing was not part of my intention), and the text of Addition IIc more serviceable as a source of intelligible lines of context for the Concordance. Letters, words, and phrases deleted by D in Addition IIc are not included in the text, but they are recorded in the critical apparatus (between square brackets); deleted entire words are also included in the Concordance (again in square brackets). The speech-prefixes—which are not concordanced—have been normalized throughout, in accordance with the "final revision" of IIc, because, as Bald notes, "C has been carefully through D's three pages, . . . frequently altering the speech-prefixes which D, who seems to have lacked a very precise knowledge of the play, has from time to time left deliberately vague" (p. 49). D's prefixes, where substantively different from those of the present text, are given in the critical apparatus.

Mine differs from Jenkins's modern-spelling text (*More*) mainly in spelling (his is naturally British) and punctuation, but we do differ in several other respects that should be noted. I have not supplied stage-directions, and I have modernized the manuscript's *argo* (l. 5) and *pumpions* (l. 16), solely because this is as far as possible a strictly modernized text; thus I also read "shrievalty" for the manuscript's *shrevaltry* (l. 42), but I retain *owed* as an *OED*-listed and in some sense "current" word in the sense 'owned,' both as Jenkins does. In lines 90-93 we differ a little more substantially (see text and critical apparatus), the focal point of the difference being in line 91, "[Let me sett vp before yor thoughts good freind$_e$] on supposytion," where Jenkins—and Chambers—read "One" and I read "On."[14] On the other hand, having prepared my text before collating Jenkins's, I was persuaded to change my "Peace! How? Peace!" (l. 28) to read, with his and Chambers's, "Peace, ho! Peace!", which seems better to fit the context but is admittedly interpretative and accordingly affects the Concordance. On "mutinies" (l. 115: MS. muty$\overset{n}{e}$s) and "momtanish" (l. 140), see the GENERAL NOTES, s.v. "*Headwords*," above.

i. The Surviving Fragment of Addition IIc's Original

Addition IIc occupies ff. 8-9^r of B.M. Harleian MS. 7368. "Fol. 9^v is blank. The scene is continued in its original form and in Munday's [S's] hand on fol. 10^r. There is a slight overlap, for the first three lines of the page (marked for omission) contain the end of More's original speech" (Greg, *IMD*, p. 214n); they correspond with lines 144-147 of Addition IIc. In *IMD*, the remainder of Scene VI—of which IIc is the first part—occupies lines 166-253 (pp. 214-218; ff. 10^{r+v} in the manuscript). The punctuation here is that of the manuscript, where the three lines divide at "punish / ment" and "graciously / pardon." Note that the original was in prose. More speaks:

> To persist in it, is present death. But if you yield yourselves,
> no doubt, what punishment you in simplicity have incurred,
> his Highness in mercy will most graciously pardon.

ii. Addition IIc

Enter Lincoln, Doll, Clown, George Betts, Williamson, Others, and a Sergeant-at-Arms.

Lincoln. Peace, hear me! He that will not see a red herring at a Harry
    groat, butter at elevenpence a pound, meal at nine shillings a
    bushel, and beef at four nobles a stone, list to me.
Betts. It will come to that pass if strangers be suffered. Mark him.
Lincoln. Our country is a great eating country, ergo they eat more in   5
    our country than they do in their own.
Clown. By a halfpenny loaf a day troy weight.
Lincoln. They bring in strange roots, which is merely to the undoing of poor
    prentices, for what's a sorry parsnip to a good heart?
Williamson. Trash, trash. They breed sore eyes, and 'tis enough to infect the 10
    city with the palsey.
Lincoln. Nay, it has infected it with the palsey, for these bastards of dung
    (as you know they grow in dung) have infected us, and it is our
    infection will make the city shake, which partly comes through
    the eating of parsnips.   15
Clown. True, and pumpkins together.
Sergeant. What say you to the mercy of the king? Do you refuse it?
Lincoln. You would have us upon th' hip, would you? No, marry, do we not; we
    accept of the king's mercy, but we will show no mercy upon
    the strangers.   20
Sergeant. You are the simplest things that ever stood in such a question.
Lincoln. How say you now, prentices? Prentices simple! Down with him!
All. Prentices simple! Prentices simple!
                  Enter the Lord Mayor, Surrey,
                       Shrewsbury.   25

Addition IIc (Modern-Spelling Text).   *C = playhouse-bookkeeper, who touched up IIc as written by D; J = Jenkins, More   s.p. = speech-prefix, and [   ] = readings deleted in the manuscript by D* (0.1) *Enter . . . Sergeant-at-Arms] Written by C, immediately below the preceding scene, on f. 7^v* (4) *s.p. Betts]* Geo Bett *C;* other *D*   (5) ergo] argo *D, J*   (7) *s.p. Clown]* betts clow *C;* other *D*   (9) [a watery] a sorry   (10) *s.p. Williamson]* willian *C;* oth *D*   (16) *s.p. Clown]* Clown. betts *C;* o *D*   pumpkins] pumpions *D, J*   (22) *How say you added in left margin in MS.*   now, prentices?] now prenty (*superscript*) *MS.; Greg:* now prenty[sses] (*IMD, p.* 209, l. 32)

78

Mayor. Hold! In the king's name, hold!

Surrey. Friends, masters, countrymen!

Mayor. Peace, ho! Peace! I charge you, keep the peace!

Shrewsbury. My masters, countrymen!

Williamson. The noble Earl of Shrewsbury, let's hear him.   30

Betts. We'll hear the Earl of Surrey.

Lincoln. The Earl of Shrewsbury.

Betts. We'll hear both.

All. Both, both, both, both!

Lincoln. Peace, I say, peace! Are you men of wisdom or   35
    what are you?

Surrey. What you will have them, but not men of wisdom.

All. We'll not hear my Lord of Surrey! No, no, no, no, no!
                       Shrewsbury, Shrewsbury!   38.1

More. Whiles they are o'er the bank of their obedience
    Thus will they bear down all things.   40

Lincoln. Shrieve More speaks. Shall we hear Shrieve More speak?

Doll. Let's hear him. A keeps a plentiful shrievalty, and a made my
    brother, Arthur Watchins, Sergeant Safe's yeoman. Let's hear
    Shrieve More.

All. Shrieve More! More! More! Shrieve More!   45

More. Even by the rule you have among yourselves,
    Command still audience.

All. Surrey, Surrey!

All. More, More!

Lincoln, Betts. Peace, peace! Silence! Peace!   50

More. You that have voice and credit with the number,
    Command them to a stillness.

Lincoln. A plague on them, they will not hold their peace. The devil
    cannot rule them.

More. Then what a rough and riotous charge have you   55
    To lead those that the devil cannot rule.
    Good masters, hear me speak!

Doll. Ay, by th' mass will we, More. Th' art a good housekeeper, and I
    thank thy good worship for my brother Arthur Watchins.

All. Peace, peace!   60

More. Look what you do offend you cry upon;
    That is, the peace. Not one of you here present,
    Had there such fellows lived when you were babes,
    That could have topped the peace, as now you would.

---

(26) s.p. *Mayor*] Maior *C;* Sher *D*   (28) ho] *J;* how *D; see "Modern-Spelling Texts" above*   [sh] charge
(30) s.p. *Williamson*] *C;* Sher *D*   (35) [ar] or   (37) [But] What   (38) [*All.*] No, no, no, no, no!   (38.1)
Shrewsbury, Shrewsbury!] Shrewsbury shr *D*   (42) shrievalty] *J;* shrevaltry *D*   (51) [mu] number

The peace wherein you have till now grown up 65
Had been ta'en from you, and the bloody times
Could not have brought you to the state of men.
Alas, poor things, what is it you have got,
Although we grant you get the thing you seek?

Betts. Marry, the removing of the strangers, which cannot choose but 70
    much advantage the poor handicrafts of the city.

More. Grant them removed, and grant that this your noise
    Hath chid down all the majesty of England.
    Imagine that you see the wretched strangers,
    Their babies at their backs, with their poor luggage 75
    Plodding to th' ports and coasts for transportation,
    And that you sit as kings in your desires,
    Authority quite silenced by your brawl,
    And you in ruff of your opinions clothed,
    What had you got? I'll tell you. You had taught 80
    How insolence and strong hand should prevail,
    How order should be quelled; and by this pattern
    Not one of you should live an aged man,
    For other ruffians as their fancies wrought,
    With selfsame hand, self reasons, and self right, 85
    Would shark on you, and men like ravenous fishes
    Would feed on one another.

Doll. Before God, that's as true as the gospel.

Lincoln. Nay, this a sound fellow, I tell you. Let's mark him.

More. Let me set up before your thoughts, good friends, 90
    On supposition—which if you will mark
    You shall perceive—how horrible a shape
    Your innovation bears. First, 'tis a sin,
    Which oft th' apostle did forewarn us of, 94a
    Urging obedience to authority, 94b
    And 'twere no error if I told you all 95a
    You were in arms 'gainst God. 95b

All. Marry, God forbid that!

More. Nay, certainly you are,
    For to the king God hath his office lent
    Of dread, of justice, power, and command;

(67) [these] the state   (71) [help] advantage   (72) your [y] noise   (75) [and] with (superscript) (79) your [yo] opinions   (87) on one] *J*; on on MS.; Greg: *"It is impossible to be certain whether D intended 'on one another' or 'one on another' "* (IMD, p. 212, l. 102n) (89) s.p. Lincoln] *C*; Betts *D*   (90) s.p. More] *C*; omit s.p. *D*   (91-92) On . . . perceive—how] One supposition, which if you will mark, / You shall perceive how *J*; see *"Modern-Spelling Texts"* above   (94) [a+b], (95) [a+b] *As Greg notes, "each pair is written as one line by D, thus completing the speech on the page,"* f. 8ᵛ *(IMD, p. 212, ll. 110-1, 112-3nn)*   (95a) [in] no

Hath bid him rule, and willed you to obey; 100
And to add ampler majesty to this,
He hath not only lent the king his figure,
His throne and sword, but given him his own name,
Calls him a god on earth. What do you then,
Rising 'gainst him that God himself installs, 105
But rise 'gainst God? What do you to your souls
In doing this, o desperate as you are?
Wash your foul minds with tears, and those same hands
That you, like rebels, lift against the peace
Lift up for peace; and your unreverent knees, 110
Make them your feet: to kneel to be forgiven
Is safer wars than ever you can make
Whose discipline is riot. Why, even your hurly
Cannot proceed but by obedience. 114a
What rebel captain, 114b
As mutinies are incident, by his name 115
Can still the rout? Who will obey a traitor?
Or how can well that proclamation sound
When there is no addition but a rebel
To qualify a rebel? You'll put down strangers,
Kill them, cut their throats, possess their houses, 120
And lead the majesty of law in lyam
To slip him like a hound. Say now the king,
As he is clement if th' offender mourn,
Should so much come too short of your great trespass
As but to banish you, whither would you go? 125
What country, by the nature of your error,
Should give you harbor? Go you to France or Flanders,
To any German province, Spain or Portugal,
Nay, anywhere that not adheres to England,
Why you must needs be strangers. Would you be pleased 130

&

(102) He [God] hath (He *added in left margin*) [le] only lent (103) and] [his] D (107) [ar] as (111)
[That] Make (112-114) Is safer...obedience *deleted by C (see n. on l. 114)* (113) why even your hurly]
in in to your obedience *written in above* [wars] hurly (114) Cannot proceed but by obedience] C
substitutes Tell me but this; Greg: "In these difficult lines, if the original writer [D] intended the interlined words in in to yo* obedienc. as a substitute for the two half-lines why euen...by obedienc (as
has been suggested) one would have expected him to delete the latter. But, with the substitution of
hurly for warrs he left the passage as it was, and must, I think, have meant it to stand. I conjecture
that a stop was intended after feet in l. 111, and that in in to yo* obedienc. should be inserted between
ryot; and why. The whole passage is clumsy but I no longer think, as I was once inclined to do, that the
author was conscious of having left it in confusion" ("Final Note on Certain Readings in Ll. 103-14," p.
[243], ll. 112-4n) (114a, 114b) so too J; as one line in MS. (115) mutinies] J; mutyes D; see General Notes,
s.v. "Headwords," above (116) [th] a traitor (122) hound. [saying] [alas alas (superscript)] Say; Greg:
"the substituted words [alas alas], interlined by D, were deleted by C" (p. [241]. l. 122n) (128) [to] Spain
(129) [why] that not

To find a nation of such barbarous temper
That, breaking out in hideous violence,
Would not afford you an abode on earth,
Whet their detested knives against your throats,
Spurn you like dogs, and, like as if that God   135
Owed not nor made not you, nor that the elements
Were not all appropriate to your comforts,
But chartered unto them? What would you think
To be thus used? This is the strangers' case,
And this your momtanish inhumanity.   140
All. Faith, a says true. Let's do as we may be done by.
Lincoln. We'll be ruled by you, Master More, if you'll stand our
    friend to procure our pardon.
More. Submit you to these noble gentlemen,
    Entreat their mediation to the king,   145
    Give up yourself to form, obey the magistrate,
    And there's no doubt but mercy may be found   147a
    If you so seek it.   147b

(137) [their] your *(superscript)* (140) momtanish] D; *see General Notes, s.v. "Headwords," above* (141)
s.p. All] With l. 140 (And this . . .) in MS. (141) Let's [us]: *ascribing the deletion to C, Greg suggests
that "the writer [D] probably intended* lett vs *but forgot to cross out the* s" *(p. [241], l. 141n)* (142)
s.p. Lincoln] C; all D (147a, 147b) *so too J; as one line in MS.* (147b) it] it *(as doubtful)* Transcription

iii. Addition III

The text given below is a modernized text of the lines in the *Tudor Facsimile*.
"This insertion is on a piece of paper pasted on to the lower part of fol. 11ᵛ, and
covering 761-96 of the deleted sc. viii a. From its position it would seem that the
addition was intended to stand at the beginning of the revised sc. viii (fol. 12ʳ) but
the necessary alteration in the S.D. has not been made, and the additional speech
has no connexion with what follows. It might of course be treated as an independ-
ent scene (cf. V), but such does not appear to have been the intention of the
scribe" (Greg, *More*, p. 79, Addition III, headnote). Bald adds that C, in whose
hand this Addition is, "could have transcribed it from a scrap of paper in D's
handwriting, just as he transcribed part of Addition V from the lines in B's handwriting on fol. 16ᵛ. But the argument for Shakespeare's authorship of this speech,
which has been asserted by various writers, depends almost entirely on stylistic
evidence. An impressive number of parallels with Shakespeare's acknowledged
work has been accumulated, and it seems reasonable, if the identity of D and
Shakespeare is granted, to accept this speech as also his" (p. 59). Bald has himself written at greater length on "Addition III of *Sir Thomas More*," as have
others.[15] Reminiscences of *Hamlet, King Lear, Othello,* and *Troilus and Cressida,*
especially, are strong indeed.

More. It is in heaven that I am thus and thus,
  And that which we profanely term our fortunes
  Is the provision of the power above,
  Fitted and shaped just to that strength of nature
  Which we are born withal. Good God, good God,   5
  That I, from such an humble bench of birth,
  Should step as 'twere up to my country's head
  And give the law out there; I, in my father's life,
  To take prerogative and tithe of knees
  From elder kinsmen, and him bind by my place   10
  To give the smooth and dexter way to me
  That owe it him by nature. Sure these things,
  Not physicked by respect, might turn our blood
  To much corruption. But More, the more thou hast,
  Either of honor, office, wealth, and calling,   15
  Which might accite thee to embrace and hug them,
  The more do thou in serpents' natures think them.
  Fear their gay skins with thought of their sharp state,
  And let this be thy maxim: to be great
  Is, when the thread of hazard is once spun,   20
  A bottom great wound up, greatly undone.

Addition III (Modern-Spelling Text). *Dyce* = Alexander Dyce, ed. Sir Thomas More, 1844; J =Jenkins
(1) *s.p. More supplied* (5) *withal Dyce, J: omit MS.* (8) *out]* Greg: "*might be ont*" (*More, p. 79, l. 9n*),
i.e., on't; C's n's and u's are virtually identical in this passage (see Tudor Facsimile) I] *A common*
Elizabethan spelling of aye. (so in Addition IIc, l. 58), which could have been intended here

iv. Concordance Materials for the Study of Addition IIc

Deleted words. All entire words written by D that are deleted in the manuscript are included
and counted in the Concordance (and Frequency List) whether they have been retained in
the modern-spelling text or not (a few deleted words have been excluded from the text,
although they are noted in the critical apparatus).[16]

Frequency List. Immediately following the Concordance is a list of words of multiple occurrence in order of frequency of occurrence. In this list, relative frequency of occurrence is
also indicated, as it is not in the Concordance proper, and both the words deleted by D
and the words of doubtful transcription are included.

Line-Numbers. The lines of the text are customarily numbered 1-147, but some of the verse-
lines in this series are in fact more than one line; namely, lines 94(a+b), 95(a+b), 114(a+b),
and 147(a+b), which are pairs of lines, or at least one full verse-line and a half-line, and
are so treated here by the use of "a" and "b" following the line-number. Thus the statistics
given at the head of the Frequency List are based on a total count of 151 lines, which

includes as "lines" the nine half-lines 40, 47, 52, 57, 87, 95b, 97, 114b, and 147b (l. 38.1 is so numbered because it is in fact written between ll. 38 and 39; it is customarily identified as part of l. 38, and it is not treated as a separate line here, except for the decimal number).

Lines of Context. The lines of context, those of the modern-spelling text given above and as numbered there, are given once only for the appropriate headword, even if the subject-word occurs more than once in the line; for example, line 2 is printed only once s.v. "A, article," although "a" occurs twice in the line (both occurrences are of course included in the total count).

1 ACCEPT

19   accept of the king's mercy, but we will show no mercy
      upon

1 ADD

101 And to add ampler majesty to this,

1 ADDITION

118 When there is no addition but a rebel

1 ADHERES

129 Nay, anywhere [why you] that not adheres to England,

1 ADVANTAGE, v.

71   much [help] advantage the poor handicrafts of the
      city.

1 AFFORD

133 Would not afford you an abode on earth,

2 AGAINST (see also "GAINST")

109 That you, like rebels, lift against the peace
134 What their detested knives against your throats,

1 AGED

83   Not one of you should live an aged man,

3 ALAS

68   Alas, poor things, what is it you have got,
122 To slip him like a hound. [saying][alas alas] Say
      now the king.

4 ALL

40   Thus will they bear down all things.
73   Hath chid down all the majesty of England.
95a And 'twere [in] no error if I told you all
137 Were not all appropriate to [their] your comforts,

1 ALTHOUGH

69   Although we grant you get the thing you seek?

---

24 A, article

1   Peace, hear me! He that will not see a red herring
      at a Harry
2   groat, butter at elevenpence a pound, meal at nine
      shillings a
5   Our country is a great eating country, ergo they eat
      more in
7   By a halfpenny loaf a day troy weight.
9   prentices, for what's [a watery] a sorry parsnip to a
      good heart?
21   You are the simplest things that ever stood in such a
      question.
42   Let's hear him. A keeps a plentiful shrievalty, and
      a made my
52   Command them to a stillness.
53   A plague on them, they will not hold their peace.
      The devil
55   Then what a rough and riotous charge have you
58   Aye, by th' mass will we, More. Th' art a good
      housekeeper, and I
89   Nay, this a sound fellow, I tell you. Let's mark him.
92   You shall perceive--how horrible a shape
93   Your innovation bears. First, 'tis a sin,
104 Calls him a god on earth. What do you then,
116 Can still the rout? Who will obey a traitor?
118 When there is no addition but a rebel
119 To qualify a rebel? You'll put down strangers,
122 To slip him like a hound. [saying][alas alas] Say
      now the king,
131 To find a nation of such barbarous temper

2 A, article

1   Peace, hear me! He that will not see a red herring
      at a Harry
3   bushel, and beef at four nobles a stone, list to me.

3 A, pron. (see also "HE")

42   Let's hear him. A keeps a plentiful shrievalty, and
      a made my
141 Faith, a says true. Let's [us] do as we may be done
      by.

1 ABODE, sb.

133 Would not afford you an abode on earth,

1 AMONG

46   Even by the rule you have among yourselves,

1 AMPLER

101   And to add ampler majesty to this,

2 AN

83   Not one of you should live an aged man,
133   Would not afford you an abode on earth.

29 AND

3   bushel, and beef at four nobles a stone, list to me.
10   Trash, trash. They breed sore eyes, and 'tis enough
      to infect the
13   (as you know they grow in dung) have infected us, and
      it is our
16   True, and pumpkins together.
42   Let's hear him. A keeps a plentiful shrievalty, and
      a made my
51   You that have voice and credit with the number,
55   Then what a rough and riotous charge have you
58   Aye, by th' mass will we, More. Th' art a good
      housekeeper, and I
66   Had been ta'en from you, and the bloody times
72   Grant them removed, and grant that this your noise
75   Their babies at their backs, [and] with their poor
      luggage
76   Plodding to th' ports and coasts for transportation,
77   And that you sit as kings in your desires,
79   And you in ruff of your opinions clothed,
81   How insolence and strong hand should prevail,
82   How order should be quelled; and by this pattern
85   With selfsame hand, self reasons, and self right,
86   Would shark on you, and men like ravenous fishes
95a   And 'twere [in] no error if I told you all
99   Of dread, of justice, power, and command;
100   Hath bid him rule, and willed you to obey;
101   And to add ampler majesty to this,
103   His throne [his] and sword, but given him his own
      name,
108   Wash your foul minds with tears, and those same hands
110   Lift up for peace; and your unreverent knees,
121   And lead the majesty of law in lyam
135   Spurn you like dogs, and, like as if that God
140   And this your montanish inhumanity.
147a And there's no doubt but mercy may be found

1 ANOTHER

87   Would feed on one another.

1 ANY

128   To any German province, [to] Spain or Portugal,

1 ANYWHERE

129   Nay, anywhere [why you] that not adheres to England,

1 APOSTLE

94a   Which oft th' apostle did forewarn us of,

1 APPROPRIATE, ppl. a.

137   Were not all appropriate to [their] your comforts,

7 ARE

21   You are the simplest things that ever stood in such a
      question.
35   Peace, I say, peace! Are you men of wisdom or
36   what are you?
39   Whiles they are o'er the bank of their obedience
97   Nay, certainly you are,
107   In doing this, o desperate as you are?
115   As mutinies are incident, by his name

1 ARMS, sb.

95b   You were in arms 'gainst God.

1 ART

58   Aye, by th' mass will we, More. Th' art a good
      housekeeper, and I

2 ARTHUR

43   brother, Arthur Watchins, Sergeant Safe's yeoman.
      Let's hear
59   thank thy good worship for my brother Arthur Watchins.

12 AS

13   (as you know they grow in dung) have infected us, and
      it is our
64   That could have topped the peace, as now you would.
77   And that you sit as kings in your desires,

86

AS
4
84 For other ruffians as their fancies wrought,
88 Before God, that's as true as the gospel.
107 In doing this, o desperate as you are?
115 As mutinies are incident, by his name
123 As he is clement if th' offender mourn,
125 As but to banish you, whither would you go?
135 Spurn you like dogs, and, like as if that God
141 Faith, a says true. Let's [us] do as we may be done by.

AT
1 Peace, hear me! He that will not see a red herring at a Harry
2 groat, butter at elevenpence a pound, meal at nine shillings a
3 bushel, and beef at four nobles a stone, list to me.
75 Their babies at their backs, [and] with their poor luggage

AT
2 groat, butter at elevenpence a pound, meal at nine shillings a

AUDIENCE
1
47 Command still audience.

AUTHORITY
1
78 Authority quite silenced by your brawl,

AUTHORITY
1
94b Urging obedience to authority,

AYE
1
58 Aye, by th' mass will we, More. Th' art a good housekeeper, and I

BABES
1
63 Had there such fellows lived when you were babes,

BABIES
1
75 Their babies at their backs, [and] with their poor luggage

BACKS, sb.
1
75 Their babies at their backs, [and] with their poor luggage

BANISH
1
125 As but to banish you, whither would you go?

BANK
1
39 Whiles they are o'er the bank of their obedience

BARBAROUS
1
131 To find a nation of such barbarous temper

BASTARDS
1
12 Nay, it has infected it with the palsey, for these bastards of dung

BE
8
82 How order should be quelled; and by this pattern
111 [That] Make them your feet: to kneel to be forgiven
130 Why you must needs be strangers. Would you be pleased
139 To be thus used? This is the strangers' case,
141 Faith, a says true. Let's [us] do as we may be done by.
142 We'll be ruled by you, Master More, if you'll stand our
147a And there's no doubt but mercy may be found

BE
1
4 It will come to that pass if strangers be suffered. Mark him.

BEAR, v.
1
40 Thus will they bear down all things.

BEARS, v.
1
93 Your innovation bears. First, 'tis a sin,

BEEF
1
3 bushel, and beef at four nobles a stone, list to me.

1 BEEN

  66 Had been ta'en from you, and the bloody times

2 BEFORE

  88 Before God, that's as true as the gospel.
  90 Let me set up before your thoughts, good friends,

1 BID, v.

  100 Hath bid him rule, and willed you to obey;

1 BLOODY

  66 Had been ta'en from you, and the bloody times

5 BOTH

  33 We'll hear both.
  34 Both, both, both, both!

1 BRAWL, sb.

  78 Authority quite silenced by your brawl,

1 BREAKING

  132 That, breaking out in hideous violence,

1 BREED, v.

  10 Trash, trash. They breed sore eyes, and 'tis enough
      to infect the

1 BRING

  8 They bring in strange roots, which is merely to the
     undoing of poor

2 BROTHER

  43 brother, Arthur Watchins, Sergeant Safe's yeoman.
     Let's hear
  59 thank thy good worship for my brother Arthur Watchins.

1 BROUGHT

  67 Could not have brought you to [these] the state of
     men.

1 BUSHEL

  3 bushel, and beef at four nobles a stone, list to me.

2 BUT, adv.

  37 [But] What you will have them, but not men of wisdom.
  125 As but to banish you, whither would you go?

7 BUT, conj.

  19 accept of the king's mercy, but we will show no mercy
     upon
  37 [But] What you will have them, but not men of wisdom.
  70 Marry, the removing of the strangers, which cannot
     choose but
  103 His throne [his] and sword, but given him his own
     name,
  106 But rise 'gainst God? What do you to your souls
  138 But chartered unto them? What would you think
  147a And there's no doubt but mercy may be found

2 BUT, prep.

  114a Cannot proceed but by obedience.
  118 When there is no addition but a rebel

1 BUTTER

  2 groat, butter at elevenpence a pound, meal at nine
     shillings a

10 BY

  7 By a halfpenny loaf a day troy weight.
  46 Even by the rule you have among yourselves,
  58 Aye, by th' mass will we, More. Th' art a good
     housekeeper, and I
  78 Authority quite silenced by your brawl,
  82 How order should be quelled; and by this pattern
  114a Cannot proceed but by obedience.
  115 As mutinies are incident, by his name
  126 What country, by the nature of your error,
  141 Faith, a says true. Let's [us] do as we may be done
     by.
  142 We'll be ruled by you, Master More, if you'll stand
     our

1 CALLS, v.

  104 Calls him a god on earth. What do you then,

3 CAN
112 Is safer wars than ever you can make
116 Can still the rout? Who will obey a traitor?
117 Or how can well that proclamation sound

4 CANNOT
54 cannot rule them.
56 To lead those that the devil cannot rule.
70 Marry, the removing of the strangers, which cannot
     choose but
114a Cannot proceed but by obedience.

1 CAPTAIN
114b What rebel captain,

1 CASE, sb.
139 To be thus used? This is the strangers' case,

1 CERTAINLY
97 Nay, certainly you are,

1 CHARGE, sb.
55 Then what a rough and riotous charge have you

1 CHARGE, v.
28 Peace, ho! Peace! I charge you, keep the peace!

1 CHARTERED
138 But chartered unto them? What would you think

1 CHID
73 Hath chid down all the majesty of England.

1 CHOOSE
70 Marry, the removing of the strangers, which cannot
     choose but

3 CITY
11 city with the palsey.
14 infection will make the city shake, which partly
     comes through

CITY
71 much [help] advantage the poor handicrafts of the
     city.

1 CLEMENT
123 As he is clement if th' offender mourn,

1 CLOTHED
79 And you in ruff of your opinions clothed,

1 COASTS, sb.
76 Plodding to th' ports and coasts for transportation,

2 COME
4 It will come to that pass if strangers be suffered.
     Mark him.
124 Should so much come too short of your great trespass

1 COMES
14 infection will make the city shake, which partly
     comes through

1 COMFORTS, sb.
137 Were not all appropriate to [their] your comforts,

1 COMMAND, sb.
99 Of dread, of justice, power, and command;

2 COMMAND, v.
47 Command still audience.
52 Command them to a stillness.

2 COULD
64 That could have topped the peace, as now you would.
67 Could not have brought you to [these] the state of
     men.

4 COUNTRY
5 Our country is a great eating country, ergo they eat
     more in
6 our country than they do in their own.

COUNTRY
126 What country, by the nature of your error,

2 COUNTRYMEN
27 Friends, masters, countrymen!
29 My masters, countrymen!

1 CREDIT, sb.
51 You that have voice and credit with the number,

1 CRY, v.
61 Look what you do offend you cry upon;

1 CUT, v.
120 Kill them, cut their throats, possess their houses,

1 DAY
7 By a halfpenny loaf a day troy weight.

1 DESIRES, sb.
77 And that you sit as kings in your desires,

1 DESPERATE
107 In doing this, o desperate as you are?

1 DETESTED
134 Whet their detested knives against your throats,

2 DEVIL
53 A plague on them, they will not hold their peace. The devil
56 To lead those that the devil cannot rule.

1 DID
94a Which oft th' apostle did forewarn us of,

1 DISCIPLINE, sb.
113 Whose discipline is riot. Why, even your [wars] hurly <in in to your obedience>

7 DO
6 our country than they do in their own.
17 What say you to the mercy of the king? Do you refuse it?
18 You would have us upon th' hip, would you? No, marry, do we not; we
61 Look what you do offend you cry upon;
104 Calls him a god on earth. What do you then,
106 But rise 'gainst God? What do you to your souls
141 Faith, a says true. Let's [us] do as we may be done by.

1 DOGS, sb.
135 Spurn you like dogs, and, like as if that God

1 DOING
107 In doing this, o desperate as you are?

1 DONE
141 Faith, a says true. Let's [us] do as we may be done by.

1 DOUBT, sb.
147a And there's no doubt but mercy may be found

4 DOWN
22 How say you now, prentices? Prentices simple! Down with him!
40 Thus will they bear down all things.
73 Hath chid down all the majesty of England.
119 To qualify a rebel? You'll put down strangers,

1 DREAD, sb.
99 Of dread, of justice, power, and command;

2 DUNG
12 Nay, it has infected it with the palsey, for these bastards of dung
13 (as you know they grow in dung) have infected us, and it is our

3 EARL
30 The noble Earl of Shrewsbury, let's hear him.
31 We'll hear the Earl of Surrey.
32 The Earl of Shrewsbury.

2 EARTH
104 Calls him a god on earth. What do you then,
133 Would not afford you an abode on earth,

1 EAT
5 Our country is a great eating country, ergo they eat more in

2 EATING
5 Our country is a great eating country, ergo they eat more in
15 the eating of parsnips.

1 ELEMENTS, sb.
136 Owed not nor made not you, nor that the elements

1 ELEVENPENCE
2 groat, butter at elevenpence a pound, meal at nine shillings a

2 ENGLAND
73 Hath chid down all the majesty of England.
129 Nay, anywhere [why you] that not adheres to England,

1 ENOUGH
10 Trash, trash. They breed sore eyes, and 'tis enough to infect the

1 ENTER
24 Enter the Lord Mayor, Surrey,

1 ENTREAT
145 Entreat their mediation to the king,

1 ERGO
5 Our country is a great eating country, ergo they eat more in

2 ERROR
95a And 'twere [in] no error if I told you all
126 What country, by the nature of your error,

1 EVEN, emphatic particle
113 Whose discipline is riot. Why, even your [wars] hurly <in in to your obedience>

1 EVEN, emphatic particle
46 Even by the rule you have among yourselves,

2 EVER
21 You are the simplest things that ever stood in such a question.
112 Is safer wars than ever you can make

1 EYES, sb.
10 Trash, trash. They breed sore eyes, and 'tis enough to infect the

1 FAITH, interj.
141 Faith, a says true. Let's [us] do as we may be done by.

1 FANCIES, sb.
84 For other ruffians as their fancies wrought,

1 FEED
87 Would feed on one another.

1 FEET
111 [That] Make them your feet: to kneel to be forgiven

1 FELLOW
89 Nay, this a sound fellow, I tell you. Let's mark him.

1 FELLOWS
63 Had there such fellows lived when you were babes,

1 FIGURE, sb.
102 He [God] hath not only lent the king his figure,

1 FIND
131 To find a nation of such barbarous temper

1 FIRST
93 Your innovation bears. First, 'tis a sin,

1 FISHES, sb.
86 Would shark on you, and men like ravenous fishes

1 FLANDERS
127 Should give you harbor? Go you to France or Flanders,

4 FOR, conj.
9 prentices, for what's [a watery] a sorry parsnip to a good heart?
12 Nay, it has infected it with the palsey, for these bastards of dung
84 For other ruffians as their fancies wrought,
98 For to the king God hath his office lent

3 FOR, prep.
59 thank thy good worship for my brother Arthur Watchins.
76 Plodding to th' ports and coasts for transportation,
110 Lift up for peace; and your unreverent knees,

1 FORBID
96 Marry, God forbid that!

1 FOREWARN
94a Which oft th' apostle did forewarn us of,

1 FORGIVEN
111 [That] Make them your feet: to kneel to be forgiven

1 FORM, sb.
146 Give up yourself to form, obey the magistrate,

1 FOUL
108 Wash your foul minds with tears, and those same hands

1 FOUND
147a And there's no doubt but mercy may be found

1 FOUR
3 bushel, and beef at four nobles a stone, list to me.

1 FRANCE
127 Should give you harbor? Go you to France or Flanders,

1 FRIEND
143 friend to procure our pardon.

2 FRIENDS
27 Friends, masters, countrymen!
90 Let me set up before your thoughts, good friends,

1 FROM
66 Had been ta'en from you, and the bloody times

3 'GAINST (see also "AGAINST")
95b You were in arms 'gainst God.
105 Rising 'gainst him that God himself installs,
106 But rise 'gainst God? What do you to your souls

1 GENTLEMEN
144 Submit you to these noble gentlemen,

1 GERMAN
128 To any German province, [to] Spain or Portugal,

1 GET
69 Although we grant you get the thing you seek?

2 GIVE
127 Should give you harbor? Go you to France or Flanders,
146 Give up yourself to form, obey the magistrate,

1 GIVEN
103 His throne [his] and sword, but given him his own
     name,

2 GO
125 As but to banish you, whither would you go?
127 Should give you harbor? Go you to France or Flanders,

8 GOD
88 Before God, that's as true as the gospel.
96 Marry, God forbid that!
98 For to the king God hath his office lent
102 He [God] hath not only lent the king his figure,
104 Calls him a god on earth. What do you then,
105 Rising 'gainst him that God himself installs,
106 But rise 'gainst God? What do you to your souls
135 Spurn you like dogs, and, like as if that God

1 GOD
95b You were in arms 'gainst God.

5 GOOD, a.
9 prentices, for what's [a watery] a sorry parsnip to a
    good heart?
57 Good masters, hear me speak!
58 Aye, by th' mass will we, More. Th' art a good
    housekeeper, and I
59 thank thy good worship for my brother Arthur Watchins.
90 Let me set up before your thoughts, good friends,

1 GOSPEL
88 Before God, that's as true as the gospel.

2 GOT
68 Alas, poor things, what is it you have got,
80 What had you got? I'll tell you. You had taught

3 GRANT, v.
69 Although we grant you get the thing you seek?
72 Grant them removed, and grant that this your noise

2 GREAT
5 Our country is a great eating country, ergo they eat
    more in
124 Should so much come too short of your great trespass

1 GROAT
2 groat, butter at elevenpence a pound, meal at nine
    shillings a

1 GROW
13 (as you know they grow in dung) have infected us, and
    it is our

1 GROWN
65 The peace wherein you have till now grown up

4 HAD
63 Had there such fellows lived when you were babes,
66 Had been ta'en from you, and the bloody times
80 What had you got? I'll tell you. You had taught

1 HALFPENNY
7 By a halfpenny loaf a day troy weight.

2 HAND
81 How insolence and strong hand should prevail,
85 With selfsame hand, self reasons, and self right,

1 HANDICRAFTS
71 much [help] advantage the poor handicrafts of the
    city.

1 HANDS
108 Wash your foul minds with tears, and those same hands

HARBOR 1

127 Should give you harbor? Go you to France or Flanders,

HARRY, sb. as a. 1

1 Peace, hear me! He that will not see a red herring
     at a Harry

HAS 1

12 Nay, it has infected it with the palsey, for these
     bastards of dung

HATH 4

73   Hath chid down all the majesty of England.
98   For to the king God hath his office lent
100 Hath bid him rule, and willed you to obey;
102 He [God] hath not only lent the king his figure,

HAVE 10

13 (as you know they grow in dung) have infected us, and
     it is our
18 You would have us upon th' hip, would you? No,
     marry, do we not; we
37 [But] What you will have them, but not men of wisdom.
46 Even by the rule you have among yourselves,
51 You that have voice and credit with the number,
55 Then what a rough and riotous charge have you
64 That could have topped the peace, as now you would.
65 The peace wherein you have till now grown up
67 Could not have brought you to [these] the state of
     men.
68 Alas, poor things, what is it you have got,

HE (see also "A, pron.") 3

1   Peace, hear me! He that will not see a red herring
       at a Harry
102 He [God] hath not only lent the king his figure,
123 As he is clement if th' offender mourn,

HEAR 9

1   Peace, hear me! He that will not see a red herring
      at a Harry
30 The noble Earl of Shrewsbury, let's hear him.
31 We'll hear the Earl of Surrey.
33 We'll hear both.
38 We'll not hear my Lord of Surrey! No, no, no, no!

HEAR

41 Shrieve More speaks. Shall we hear Shrieve More
      speak?
42 Let's hear him. A keeps a plentiful shrievalty, and
      a made my
43 brother, Arthur Watchins, Sergeant Safe's yeoman.
      Let's hear.
57 Good masters, hear me speak!

HEART 1

9 prentices, for what's [a watery] a sorry parsnip to a
     good heart?

HELP, v. 1

71 much [help] advantage the poor handicrafts of the
     city.

HERE 1

62 That is, the peace. Not one of you here present,

HERRING 1

1 Peace, hear me! He that will not see a red herring
     at a Harry

HIDEOUS 1

132 That, breaking out in hideous violence,

HIM 10

4   It will come to that pass if strangers be suffered.
       Mark him.
22   How say you now, prentices? Prentices simple! Down
       with him!
30   The noble Earl of Shrewsbury, let's hear him.
42   Let's hear him. A keeps a plentiful shrievalty, and
       a made my
89   Nay, this a sound fellow, I tell you. Let's mark him.
100 Hath bid him rule, and willed you to obey;
103 His throne [his] and sword, but given him his own
       name.
104 Calls him a god on earth. What do you then,
105 Rising 'gainst him that God himself installs,
122 To slip him like a hound. [saying] [alas alas] say
       now the king,

IN

95a And 'twere [in] no error if I told you all
95b You were in arms 'gainst God.
107 In doing this, o desperate as you are?
113 Whose discipline is riot. Why, even your [wars]
121 And lead the majesty of law in lyam
132 That, breaking out in hideous violence,

1 INCIDENT, a.

115 As mutinies are incident, by his name

1 INFECT

10   Trash, trash. They breed sore eyes, and 'tis enough
     to infect the

2 INFECTED

12   Nay, it has infected it with the palsey, for these
     bastards of dung
13   (as you know they grow in dung) have infected us, and
     it is our

1 INFECTION

14   infection will make the city shake, which partly
     comes through

1 INHUMANITY

140 And this your momtanish inhumanity.

1 INNOVATION

93   Your innovation bears. First, 'tis a sin,

1 INSOLENCE

81   How insolence and strong hand should prevail,

1 INSTALLS

105 Rising 'gainst him that God himself installs,

10 IS

5   Our country is a great eating country, ergo they eat
     more in
8   They bring in strange roots, which is merely to the
     undoing of poor

IS

13   (as you know they grow in dung) have infected us, and
     it is our
62   That is, the peace. Not one of you here present,
68   Alas, poor things, what is it you have got,
112 Is safer wars than ever you can make
113 Whose discipline is riot. Why, even your [wars]
118 When there is no addition but a rebel
123 As he is clement if th' offender mourn,
139 To be thus used? This is the strangers' case,

7 IT

4   It will come to that pass if strangers be suffered.
     Mark him.
12   Nay, it has infected it with the palsey, for these
     bastards of dung
13   (as you know they grow in dung) have infected us, and
     it is our
17   What say you to the mercy of the king? Do you refuse
     it?
68   Alas, poor things, what is it you have got,
147b If you so seek it.

1 JUSTICE

99   Of dread, of justice, power, and command;

1 KEEP

28   Peace, ho! Peace! I charge you, keep the peace!

1 KEEPS

42   Let's hear him. A keeps a plentiful shrievalty, and
     a made my

1 KILL

120 Kill them, cut their throats, possess their houses,

5 KING

17   What say you to the mercy of the king? Do you refuse
     it?
98   For the king God hath his office lent
102 He [God] hath not only lent the king his figure,
122 To slip him like a hound. [saying][alas alas] Say
     now the king,
145 Entreat their mediation to the king,

LYAM
1
121 And lead the majesty of law in lyam

MADE
2
42 Let's hear him. A keeps a plentiful shrievalty, and
   a made my
136 Owed not nor made not you, nor that the elements

MAGISTRATE
1
146 Give up yourself to form, obey the magistrate,

MAJESTY
3
73 Hath chid down all the majesty of England.
101 And to add ampler majesty to this,
121 And lead the majesty of law in lyam

MAKE
3
14 infection will make the city shake, which partly
   comes through
111 [That] Make them your feet: to kneel to be forgiven
112 Is safer wars than ever you can make

MAN
1
83 Not one of you you should live an aged man,

MARK, v.
3
4 It will come to that pass if strangers be suffered.
  Mark him.
89 Nay, this a sound fellow, I tell you. Let's mark him.
91 On supposition—which if you will mark

MARRY, interj.
3
18 You would have us upon th' hip, would you? No,
   marry, do we not; we
70 Marry, the removing of the strangers, which cannot
   choose but
96 Marry, God forbid that!

MASS, sb. (oath)
1
58 Aye, by th' mass will we, More. Th' art a good
   housekeeper, and I

MASTER, sb.
1
142 We'll be ruled by you, Master More, if you'll stand
    our

MASTERS, sb.
3
27 Friends, masters, countrymen!
29 My masters, countrymen!
57 Good masters, hear me speak!

MAY, v.
2
141 Faith, a says true. Let's [us] do as we may be done
     by.
147a And there's no doubt but mercy may be found

MAYOR
1
24 Enter the Lord Mayor, Surrey,

ME
4
1 Peace, hear me! He that will not see a red herring
  at a Harry
3 bushel, and beef at four nobles a stone, list to me.
57 Good masters, hear me speak!
90 Let me set up before your thoughts, good friends,

MEAL
1
2 groat, butter at elevenpence a pound, meal at nine
  shillings a

MEDIATION
1
145 Entreat their mediation to the king,

MEN
4
35 Peace, I say, peace! Are you men of wisdom or
37 [But] What you will have them, but not men of wisdom.
67 Could not have brought you to [these] the state of
   men.
86 Would shark on you, and men like ravenous fishes

MERCY
4
17 What say you to the mercy of the king? Do you refuse
   it?
19 accept of the king's mercy, but we will show no mercy
   upon

MERCY
1
147a And there's no doubt but mercy may be found

MERELY
1
8 They bring in strange roots, which is merely to the
undoing of poor

MINDS
1
108 Wash your foul minds with tears, and those same hands

MONTANISH
1
140 And this your montanish inhumanity.

MORE, a.
1
5 Our country is a great eating country, ergo they eat
more in

MORE, personal name
11
41 Shrieve More speaks. Shall we hear Shrieve More
speak?
44 Shrieve More.
45 Shrieve More! More! Shrieve More!
49 More, More!
58 Aye, by th' mass will we, More. Th' art a good
housekeeper, and I
142 We'll be ruled by you, Master More, if you'll stand
our

MOURN
1
123 As he is clement if th' offender mourn,

MUCH
2
71 much [help] advantage the poor handicrafts of the
city.
124 Should so much come too short of your great trespass

MUST
1
130 Why you must needs be strangers. Would you be pleased

MUTINIES, sb.
1
115 As mutinies are incident, by his name

4 MY
29 My masters, countrymen!
38 We'll not hear my Lord of Surrey! No, no, no, no!
42 Let's hear him. A keeps a plentiful shrievalty, and
a made my
59 thank thy good worship for my brother Arthur Watchins.

3 NAME, sb.
26 Hold! In the king's name, hold!
103 His throne [his] and sword, but given him his own
name,
115 As mutinies are incident, by his name

1 NATION
131 To find a nation of such barbarous temper

1 NATURE
126 What country, by the nature of your error,

4 NAY
12 Nay, it has infected it with the palsey, for these
bastards of dung
89 Nay, this a sound fellow, I tell you. Let's mark him.
97 Nay, certainly you are,
129 Nay, anywhere [why you] that not adheres to England,

1 NEEDS, adv.
130 Why you must needs be strangers. Would you be pleased

1 NINE
2 groat, butter at elevenpence a pound, meal at nine
shillings a

10 NO
18 You would have us upon th' hip, would you? No,
marry, do we not; we
19 accept of the king's mercy, but we will show no mercy
upon
38 We'll not hear my Lord of Surrey! No, no, no, no!
95a And 'twere [in] no error if I told you all
118 When there is no addition but a rebel
147a And there's no doubt but mercy may be found

2 NOBLE, a.
    30   The noble Earl of Shrewsbury, let's hear him.
    144 Submit you to these noble gentlemen,

1 NOBLES, sb. (coins)
    3   bushel, and beef at four nobles a stone, list to me.

1 NOISE
    72   Grant them removed, and grant that this your noise

2 NOR
    136 Owed not nor made not you, nor that the elements

14 NOT
    1   Peace, hear me! He that will not see a red herring
         at a Harry
    18   You would have us upon th' hip, would you? No,
         marry, do we not; we
    37   [But] What you will have them, but not men of wisdom.
    38   We'll not hear my Lord of Surrey! No, no, no, no, no!
    53   A plague on them, they will not hold their peace.
         The devil
    62   That is, the peace. Not one of you here present,
    67   Could not have brought you to [these] the state of
         men.
    83   Not one of you should live an aged man,
    102 He [God] hath not only lent the king his figure,
    129 Nay, anywhere [why you] that not adheres to England,
    133 Would not afford you an abode on earth,
    136 Owed not nor made not you, nor that the elements
    137 Were not all appropriate to [their] your comforts,

4 NOW
    22   How say you now, prentices? Prentices simple! Down
         with him!
    64   That could have topped the peace, as now you would.
    65   The peace wherein you have till now grown up
    122 To slip him like a hound. [saying] [alas alas] Say
         now the king,

1 NUMBER, sb.
    51   You that have voice and credit with the number,

1 O
    107 In doing this, o desperate as you are?

4 OBEDIENCE
    39   Whiles they are o'er the bank of their obedience
    94b Urging obedience to authority,
    113 Whose discipline is riot. Why, even your [wars]
         hurly <in in to your obedience>
    114a Cannot proceed but by obedience.

3 OBEY
    100 Hath bid him rule, and willed you to obey;
    116 Can still the rout? Who will obey a traitor?
    146 Give up yourself to form, obey the magistrate,

1 O'ER
    39   Whiles they are o'er the bank of their obedience

26 OF
    8   They bring in strange roots, which is merely to the
         undoing of poor
    12   Nay, it has infected it with the palsey, for these
         bastards of dung
    15   the eating of parsnips.
    17   What say you to the mercy of the king? Do you refuse
         it?
    19   accept of the king's mercy, but we will show no mercy
         upon
    30   The noble Earl of Shrewsbury, let's hear him.
    31   We'll hear the Earl of Surrey.
    32   The Earl of Shrewsbury.
    35   Peace, I say, peace! Are you men of wisdom or
    37   [But] What you will have them, but not men of wisdom.
    38   We'll not hear my Lord of Surrey! No, no, no, no!
    39   Whiles they are o'er the bank of their obedience
    62   That is, the peace. Not one of you here present,
    67   Could not have brought you to [these] the state of
         men.
    70   Marry, the removing of the strangers, which cannot
         choose but
    71   much [help] advantage the poor handicrafts of the
         city.
    73   Hath chid down all the majesty of England.
    79   And you in ruff of your opinions clothed,
    83   Not one of you should live an aged man,
    94a Which oft th' apostle did forewarn us of,
    99   Of dread, of justice, power, and command;

OF

121 And lead the majesty of law in lyam
124 Should so much come too short of your great trespass
126 What country, by the nature of your error,
131 To find a nation of such barbarous temper

1 OFFEND

61 Look what you do offend you cry upon;

1 OFFENDER

123 As he is clement if th' offender mourn,

1 OFFICE

98 For to the king God hath his office lent

1 OFT

94a Which oft th' apostle did forewarn us of,

6 ON

53 A plague on them, they will not hold their peace.
    The devil
86 Would shark on you, and men like ravenous fishes
87 Would feed on one another.
91 On supposition--which if you will mark
104 Calls him a god on earth. What do you then,
133 Would not afford you an abode on earth.

2 ONE

83 Not one of you should live an aged man,
87 Would feed on one another.

1 ONE

62 That is, the peace. Not one of you here present,

1 ONLY

102 He [God] hath not only lent the king his figure,

1 OPINIONS

79 And you in ruff of your opinions clothed,

---

4 OR

35 Peace, I say, peace! Are you men of wisdom or
117 Or how can well that proclamation sound
127 Should give you harbor? Go you to France or Flanders,
128 To any German province, [to] Spain or Portugal,

1 ORDER

82 How order should be quelled; and by this pattern

1 OTHER

84 For other ruffians as their fancies wrought,

5 OUR

5 Our country is a great eating country, ergo they eat
    more in
6 our country than they do in their own.
13 (as you know they grow in dung) have infected us, and
    it is our
142 We'll be ruled by you, Master More, if you'll stand
    our
143 friend to procure our pardon.

1 OUT

132 That, breaking out in hideous violence,

1 OWED

136 Owed not nor made not you, nor that the elements

2 OWN, a.

6 our country than they do in their own.
103 His throne [his] and sword, but given him his own
    name,

2 PALSEY

11 city with the palsey.
12 Nay, it has infected it with the palsey, for these
    bastards of dung

1 PARDON, sb.

143 friend to procure our pardon.

PRESENT, a.
1
62 That is, the peace. Not one of you here present,

PREVAIL
1
81 How insolence and strong hand should prevail,

PROCEED
1
114a Cannot proceed but by obedience.

PROCLAMATION
1
117 Or how can well that proclamation sound

PROCURE
1
143 friend to procure our pardon.

PROVINCE
1
128 To any German province, [to] Spain or Portugal,

PUMPKINS
1
16 True, and pumpkins together.

PUT
1
119 To qualify a rebel? You'll put down strangers,

QUALIFY
1
119 To qualify a rebel? You'll put down strangers,

QUELLED
1
82 How order should be quelled; and by this pattern

QUESTION, sb.
1
21 You are the simplest things that ever stood in such a
       question.

QUITE
1
78 Authority quite silenced by your brawl,

RAVENOUS
1
86 Would shark on you, and men like ravenous fishes

REASONS, sb.
1
85 With selfsame hand, self reasons, and self right,

REBEL, sb.
3
114b What rebel captain,
118 When there is no addition but a rebel
119 To qualify a rebel? You'll put down strangers,

REBELS, sb.
1
109 That you, like rebels, lift against the peace

RED
1
1 Peace, hear me! He that will not see a red herring
       at a Harry

REFUSE, v.
1
17 What say you to the mercy of the king? Do you refuse
       it?

REMOVED
1
72 Grant them removed, and grant that this your noise

REMOVING
1
70 Marry, the removing of the strangers, which cannot
       choose but

RIGHT, sb.
1
85 With selfsame hand, self reasons, and self right,

RIOT, sb.
1
113 Whose discipline is riot. Why, even your [wars]
       hurly <in in to your obedience>

RIOTOUS
1
55 Then what a rough and riotous charge have you

104

1 SHAKE
14 infection will make the city shake, which partly
   comes through

2 SHALL
41 Shrieve More speaks. Shall we hear Shrieve More
   speak?
92 You shall perceive--how horrible a shape

1 SHAPE, sb.
92 You shall perceive--how horrible a shape

1 SHARK, v.
86 Would shark on you, and men like ravenous fishes

1 SHILLINGS
2 groat, butter at elevenpence a pound, meal at nine
   shillings a

1 SHORT
124 Should so much come too short of your great trespass

5 SHOULD
81 How insolence and strong hand should prevail,
82 How order should be quelled; and by this pattern
83 Not one of you should live an aged man,
124 Should so much come too short of your great trespass
127 Should give you harbor? Go you to France or Flanders,

1 SHOW, v.
19 accept of the king's mercy, but we will show no mercy
   upon

5 SHREWSBURY, personal name
25 Shrewsbury.
30 The noble Earl of Shrewsbury.
32 The Earl of Shrewsbury.
38.1 Shrewsbury, Shrewsbury!

1 SHRIEVALTY
42 Let's hear him. A keeps a plentiful shrievalty, and
   a made my

5 SHRIEVE
41 Shrieve More speaks. Shall we hear Shrieve More
   speak?
44 Shrieve More.
45 Shrieve More! More! More! Shrieve More!

1 SILENCE, v. (interj.)
50 Peace, peace! Silence! Peace!

1 SILENCED
78 Authority quite silenced by your brawl,

3 SIMPLE
22 How say you now, prentices? Prentices simple! Down
   with him!
23 Prentices simple! Prentices simple!

1 SIMPLEST
21 You are the simplest things that ever stood in such a
   question.

1 SIN, sb.
93 Your innovation bears. First, 'tis a sin,

1 SIT
77 And that you sit as kings in your desires,

1 SLIP
122 To slip him like a hound. [saying] [alas alas] Say
   now the king,

2 SO
124 Should so much come too short of your great trespass
147b If you so seek it.

1 SORE, a.
10 Trash, trash. They breed sore eyes, and 'tis enough
   to infect the

SORRY
1
9   prentices, for what's [a watery] a sorry parsnip to a
       good heart?

SOULS
1
106   But rise 'gainst God? What do you to your souls

SOUND, a.
1
89   Nay, this a sound fellow, I tell you. Let's mark him.

SOUND, v.
1
117   Or how can well that proclamation sound

SPAIN
1
128   To any German province, [to] Spain or Portugal,

SPEAK
2
41   Shrieve More speaks. Shall we hear Shrieve More
       speak?
57   Good masters, hear me speak!

SPEAKS
1
41   Shrieve More speaks. Shall we hear Shrieve More
       speak?

SPURN
1
135   Spurn you like dogs, and, like as if that God

STAND, v.
1
142   We'll be ruled by you, Master More, if you'll stand
       our

STATE, sb.
1
67   Could not have brought you to [these] the state of
       men.

STILL, a.
1
47   Command still audience.

STILL, v.
1
116   Can still the rout? Who will obey a traitor?

STILLNESS
1
52   Command them to a stillness.

STONE, sb.
1
3   bushel, and beef at four nobles a stone, list to me.

STOOD
1
21   You are the simplest things that ever stood in such a
       question.

STRANGE
1
8   They bring in strange roots, which is merely to the
       undoing of poor

STRANGERS
5
20   the strangers.
70   Marry, the removing of the strangers, which cannot
       choose but
74   Imagine that you see the wretched strangers,
119   To qualify a rebel? You'll put down strangers,
130   Why you must needs be strangers. Would you be pleased

STRANGERS
1
4   It will come to that pass if strangers be suffered.
       Mark him.

STRANGERS'
1
139   To be thus used? This is the strangers' case,

STRONG
1
81   How insolence and strong hand should prevail,

SUBMIT
1
144   Submit you to these noble gentlemen,

SUCH
3
21   You are the simplest things that ever stood in such a
       question.

SUCH

63   Had there such fellows lived when you were babes,
131 To find a nation of such barbarous temper

1 SUFFERED

4   It will come to that pass if strangers be suffered.
     Mark him.

1 SUPPOSITION

91   On supposition--which if you will mark

5 SURREY, personal name

24   Enter the Lord Mayor, Surrey,
31   We'll hear the Earl of Surrey.
38   We'll not hear my Lord of Surrey! No, no, no, no!
48   Surrey, Surrey!

1 SWORD

103 His throne [his] and sword, but given him his own
     name,

1 TA'EN

66   Had been ta'en from you, and the bloody times

1 TAUGHT

80   What had you got? I'll tell you. You had taught

1 TEARS, sb.

108 Wash your foul minds with tears, and those same hands

2 TELL

80   What had you got? I'll tell you. You had taught
89   Nay, this a sound fellow, I tell you. Let's mark him.

1 TEMPER, sb.

131 To find a nation of such barbarous temper

6 TH', contr. (THE)

18   You would have us upon th' hip, would you? No,
     marry, do we not; we
58   Aye, by th' mass will we, More. Th' art a good
     housekeeper, and I

TH', contr. (THE)

76   Plodding to th' ports and coasts for transportation,
94a Which oft th' apostle did forewarn us of,
123 As he is clement if th' offender mourn,

2 THAN

6   our country than they do in their own.
112 Is safer wars than ever you can make

1 THANK

59   thank thy good worship for my brother Arthur Watchins.

2 THAT, a.

4   It will come to that pass if strangers be suffered.
     Mark him.
117 Or how can well that proclamation sound

5 THAT, conj.

72   Grant them removed, and grant that this your noise
74   Imagine that you see the wretched strangers,
77   And that you sit as kings in your desires,
135 Spurn you like dogs, and, like as if that God
136 Owed not nor made not you, nor that the elements

12 THAT, pron.

1   Peace, hear me! He that will not see a red herring
     at a Harry
21   You are the simplest things that ever stood in such a
     question.
51   You that have voice and credit with the number,
56   To lead those that the devil cannot rule.
62   That is, the peace. Not one of you here present,
64   That could have topped the peace, as now you would.
96   Marry, God forbid that!
105 Rising 'gainst him that God himself installs,
109 That you, like rebels, lift against the peace
111 [That] Make them your feet: to kneel to be forgiven
129 Nay, anywhere [why you] that not adheres to England,
132 That, breaking out in hideous violence,

1 THAT'S, comp. contr.

88   Before God, that's as true as the gospel.

107

45 THE

8   They bring in strange roots, which is merely to the
10   undoing of poor
     Trash, trash. They breed sore eyes, and 'tis enough
11   to infect the
     city with the palsey.
12   Nay, it has infected it with the palsey, for these
     bastards of dung
14   infection will make the city shake, which partly
     comes through
15   the eating of parsnips.
17   What say you to the mercy of the king? Do you refuse
     it?
19   accept of the king's mercy, but we will show no mercy
     upon
20   the strangers.
21   You are the simplest things that ever stood in such a
     question.
24   Enter the Lord Mayor, Surrey,
26   Hold! In the king's name, hold!
28   Peace, ho! Peace! I charge you, keep the peace!
30   Well hear the Earl of Shrewsbury, let's hear him.
31   We'll hear the Earl of Surrey.
32   The Earl of Shrewsbury.
39   Whiles they are o'er the bank of their obedience
46   Even by the rule you have among yourselves,
51   You that have voice and credit with the number,
53   A plague on them, they will not hold their peace.
     The devil
56   To lead those that the devil cannot rule.
62   That is, the peace. Not one of you here present,
64   That could have topped the peace, as now you would.
65   The peace wherein you have till now grown up
66   Had been ta'en from you, and the bloody times
67   Could not have brought you to [these] the state of
     men.
69   Although we grant you get the thing you seek?
70   Marry, the removing of the strangers, which cannot
     choose but
71   much [help] advantage the poor handicrafts of the
     city.
73   Hath chid down all the majesty of England.
74   Imagine that you see the wretched strangers,
88   Before God, that's as true as the gospel.
98   For to the king God hath his office lent
102 He [God] hath not only lent the king his figure,
109 That you, like rebels, lift against the peace
116 Can still the rout? Who will obey a traitor?
121 And lead the majesty of law in lyam
122 To slip him like a hound. [saying] [alas alas] Say
     now the king,

THE

126 What country, by the nature of your error,
136 Owed not nor made not you, nor that the elements
139 To be thus used? This is the strangers' case,
145 Entreat their mediation to the king,
146 Give up yourself to form, obey the magistrate,

1 THE

17   What say you to the mercy of the king? Do you refuse
     it?

12 THEIR

6   our country than they do in their own.
39   Whiles they are o'er the bank of their obedience
53   A plague on them, they will not hold their peace.
     The devil
75   Their babies at their backs, [and] with their poor
     luggage
84   For other ruffians as their fancies wrought,
120 Kill them, cut their throats, possess their houses,
134 Whet their detested knives against your throats,
137 Were not all appropriate to [their] your comforts,
145 Entreat their mediation to the king,

8 THEM

37   [But] What you will have them, but not men of wisdom.
52   Command them to a stillness.
53   A plague on them, they will not hold their peace.
     The devil
54   cannot rule them.
72   Grant them removed, and grant that this your noise
111 [That] Make them your feet: to kneel to be forgiven
120 Kill them, cut their throats, possess their houses,
138 But chartered unto them? What would you think

2 THEN

55   Then what a rough and riotous charge have you
104 Calls him a god on earth. What do you then,

2 THERE

63   Had there such fellows lived when you were babes,
118 When there is no addition but a rebel

108

THIS, pron.

139 To be thus used? This is the strangers' case,
140 And this your momtanish inhumanity.

1 THIS, pron.; comp. contr.

89   Nay, this a sound fellow, I tell you. Let's mark him.

2 THOSE

56   To lead those that the devil cannot rule.
108 Wash your foul minds with tears, and those same hands

1 THOUGHTS

90   Let me set up before your thoughts, good friends,

2 THROATS

120 Kill them, cut their throats, possess their houses,
134 Whet their detested knives against your throats,

1 THRONE

103 His throne [his] and sword, but given him his own
       name,

1 THROUGH

14   infection will make the city shake, which partly
       comes through

2 THUS

40   Thus will they bear down all things.
139 To be thus used? This is the strangers' case,

1 THY

59   thank thy good worship for my brother Arthur Watchins.

1 TILL

65   The peace wherein you have till now grown up

1 TIMES

66   Had been ta'en from you, and the bloody times

1 THERE'S

147a And there's no doubt but mercy may be found

3 THESE

12   Nay, it has infected it with the palsey, for these
       bastards of dung
67   Could not have brought you to [these] the state of
       men.
144 Submit you to these noble gentlemen,

8 THEY

5   Our country is a great eating country, ergo they eat
       more in
6   our country than they do in their own.
8   They bring in strange roots, which is merely to the
       undoing of poor
10   Trash, trash. They breed sore eyes, and 'tis enough
       to infect the
13   (as you know they grow in dung) have infected us, and
       it is our
39   Whiles they are o'er the bank of their obedience
40   Thus will they bear down all things.
53   A plague on them, they will not hold their peace.
       The devil

1 THING

69   Although we grant you get the thing you seek?

3 THINGS

21   You are the simplest things that ever stood in such a
       question.
40   Thus will they bear down all things.
68   Alas, poor things, what is it you have got,

1 THINK

138 But chartered unto them? What would you think

1 THIS, a.

82   How order should be quelled; and by this pattern

5 THIS, pron.

72   Grant them removed, and grant that this your noise
101 And to add ampler majesty to this,
107 In doing this, o desperate as you are?

2 'TIS

10   Trash, trash. They breed sore eyes, and 'tis enough
     to infect the
93   Your innovation bears. First, 'tis a sin,

33 TO

3   bushel, and beef at four nobles a stone, list to me.
4   It will come to that pass if strangers be suffered.
8   They bring in strange roots, which is merely to the
     undoing of poor
9   prentices, for what's [a watery] a sorry parsnip to a
     good heart?
10   Trash, trash. They breed sore eyes, and 'tis enough
     to infect the
17   What say you to the mercy of the king? Do you refuse
     it?
52   Command them to a stillness.
56   To lead those that the devil cannot rule.
67   Could not have brought you to [these] the state of
     men:
76   Plodding to th' ports and coasts for transportation,
94b Urging obedience to authority,
98   For to the King God hath his office lent
100 Hath bid him rule, and willed you to obey;
101 And to add ampler majesty to this,
106 But rise 'gainst God? What do you to your souls
111 [That] Make them your feet: to kneel to be forgiven
113 Whose discipline is riot. Why, even your [wars]
     hurly <in in to your obedience>
119 To qualify a rebel? You'll put down strangers,
122 To slip him like a hound. [saying] [alas alas] Say
     now the king,
125 As but to banish you, whither would you go?
127 Should give you harbor? Go you to France or Flanders,
128 To any German province, [to] Spain or Portugal,
129 Nay, anywhere [why you] that not adheres to England,
131 To find a nation of such barbarous temper
137 Were not all appropriate to [their] your comforts,
139 To be thus used? This is the strangers' case;
143 friend to procure our pardon.
144 Submit you to these noble gentlemen,
145 Entreat their mediation to the king,
146 Give up yourself to form, obey the magistrate,

1 TOGETHER

16   True, and pumpkins together.

1 TOLD

95a And 'twere [in] no error if I told you all

1 TOO

124 Should so much come too short of your great trespass

1 TOPPED

64   That could have topped the peace, as now you would.

1 TRAITOR

116 Can still the rout? Who will obey a traitor?

1 TRANSPORTATION

76   Plodding to th' ports and coasts for transportation,

2 TRASH, sb.

10   Trash, trash. They breed sore eyes, and 'tis enough
     to infect the

1 TRESPASS, sb

124 Should so much come too short of your great trespass

1 TROY

7   By a halfpenny loaf a day troy weight.

1 TRUE, a.

88   Before God, that's as true as the gospel.

2 TRUE, adv.

16   True, and pumpkins together.
141 Faith, a says true. Let's [us] do as we may be done
     by.

1 'TWERE

95a And 'twere [in] no error if I told you all

1 UNDOING, vbl. sb.

8   They bring in strange roots, which is merely to the
     undoing of poor

1 WELL

117 Or how can well that proclamation sound

3 WERE

63 Had there such fellows lived when you were babes,
95b You were in arms 'gainst God.
137 Were not all appropriate to [their] your comforts,

12 WHAT

17 What say you to the mercy of the king? Do you refuse it?
36 what are you?
37 [But] What you will have them, but not men of wisdom.
55 Then what a rough and riotous charge have you
61 Look what you do offend you cry upon;
68 Alas, poor things, what is it you have got,
80 What had you got? I'll tell you. You had taught
104 Calls him a god on earth. What do you then,
106 But rise 'gainst God? What do you to your souls
114b What rebel captain,
126 What country, by the nature of your error,
138 But chartered unto them? What would you think

1 WHAT'S, comp. contr.

9 prentices, for what's [a watery] a sorry parsnip to a good heart?

2 WHEN

63 Had there such fellows lived when you were babes,
118 When there is no addition but a rebel

1 WHEREIN

65 The peace wherein you have till now grown up

1 WHET

134 Whet their detested knives against your throats,

5 WHICH

8 They bring in strange roots, which is merely to the undoing of poor
14 infection will make the city shake, which partly comes through
70 Marry, the removing of the strangers, which cannot choose but

WHICH

91 On supposition—which if you will mark
94a Which oft th' apostle did forewarn us of,

1 WHILES

39 Whiles they are o'er the bank of their obedience

1 WHITHER

125 As but to banish you, whither would you go?

1 WHO

116 Can still the rout? Who will obey a traitor?

1 WHOSE

113 Whose discipline is riot. Why, even your [wars] hurly <in in to your obedience>

3 WHY

113 Whose discipline is riot. Why, even your [wars] hurly <in in to your obedience>
129 Nay, anywhere [why you] that not adheres to England,
130 Why you must needs be strangers. Would you be pleased

10 WILL, v.

1 Peace, hear me! He that will not see a red herring at a Harry
4 It will come to that pass if strangers be suffered. Mark him.
14 infection will make the city shake, which partly comes through
19 accept of the king's mercy, but we will show no mercy upon
37 [But] What you will have them, but not men of wisdom.
40 Thus will they bear down all things.
53 A plague on them, they will not hold their peace. The devil
58 Aye, by th' mass will we, More. Th' art a good housekeeper, and I
91 On supposition—which if you will mark
116 Can still the rout? Who will obey a traitor?

1 WILLED

100 Hath bid him rule, and willed you to obey;

YOU

18 You would have us upon th' hip, would you? No,
    marry, do we not; we
21 You are the simplest things that ever stood in such a
    question.
22 How say you now, prentices? Prentices simple! Down
    with him!
28 Peace, ho! Peace! I charge you, keep the peace!
35 Peace, I say, peace! Are you men of wisdom or
36 what are you?
37 [But] What you will have them, but not men of wisdom.
46 Even by the rule you have among yourselves,
51 You that have voice and credit with the number,
55 Then what a rough and riotous charge have you
61 Look what you do offend you cry upon;
62 That is, the peace. Not one of you here present,
63 Had there such fellows lived when you were babes,
64 That could have topped the peace, as now you would.
65 The peace wherein you have till now grown up
66 Had been ta'en from you, and the bloody times
67 Could not have brought you to [these] the state of
    men.
68 Alas, poor things, what is it you have got,
69 Although we grant you get the thing you seek?
74 Imagine that you see the wretched strangers,
77 And that you sit as kings in your desires,
79 And you in ruff of your opinions clothed,
80 What had you got? I'll tell you. You had taught
83 Not one of you should live an aged man,
86 Would shark on you, and men like ravenous fishes
89 Nay, this a sound fellow, I tell you. Let's mark him.
91 On supposition--which if you will mark
92 You shall perceive--how horrible a shape
95a And 'twere [in] no error if I told you all
95b You were in arms 'gainst God.
97 Nay, certainly you are,
100 Hath bid him rule, and willed you to obey;
104 Calls him a god on earth. What do you then,
106 But rise 'gainst God? What do you to your souls
107 In doing this, o desperate as you are?
109 That you, like rebels, lift against the peace
112 Is safer wars than ever you can make
125 As but to banish you, whither would you go?
127 Should give you harbor? Go you to France or Flanders,
129 Nay, anywhere [why you] that not adheres to England,
130 Why you must needs be strangers. Would you be pleased
133 Would not afford you an abode on earth,
135 Spurn you like dogs, and, like as if that God
136 Owed not nor made not you, nor that the elements
138 But chartered unto them? What would you think
142 We'll be ruled by you, Master More, if you'll stand
    our

2 WISDOM

35 Peace, I say, peace! Are you men of wisdom or
37 [But] What you will have them, but not men of wisdom.

7 WITH

11 city with the palsey.
12 Nay, it has infected it with the palsey, for these
    bastards of dung
22 How say you now, prentices? Prentices simple! Down
    with him!
51 You that have voice and credit with the number,
75 Their babies at their backs, [and] with their poor
    luggage
85 With selfsame hand, self reasons, and self right,
108 Wash your foul minds with tears, and those same hands

1 WORSHIP, sb.

59 thank thy good worship for my brother Arthur Watchins.

9 WOULD

18 You would have us upon th' hip, would you? No,
    marry, do we not; we
64 That could have topped the peace, as now you would.
86 Would shark on you, and men like ravenous fishes
87 Would feed on one another.
125 As but to banish you, whither would you go?
130 Why you must needs be strangers. Would you be pleased
133 Would not afford you an abode on earth,
138 But chartered unto them? What would you think

1 WRETCHED

74 Imagine that you see the wretched strangers,

1 WROUGHT, v.

84 For other ruffians as their fancies wrought,

1 YEOMAN

43 brother, Arthur Watchins, Sergeant Safe's yeoman.
    Let's hear

59 YOU

13 (as you know they grow in dung) have infected us, and
    it is our
17 What say you to the mercy of the king? Do you refuse
    it?

YOU

144 Submit you to these noble gentlemen,
147b If you so seek it.

2 YOU'LL

119 To qualify a rebel? You'll put down strangers,
142 We'll be ruled by you, Master More, if you'll stand
     our

17 YOUR

72   Grant them removed, and grant that this your noise
77   And that you sit as kings in your desires,
78   Authority quite silenced by your brawl,
79   And you in ruff of your opinions clothed,
90   Let me set up before your thoughts, good friends,
93   Your innovation bears. First, 'tis a sin,
106 But rise 'gainst God? What do you to your souls
108 Wash your foul minds with tears, and those same hands
110 Lift up for peace; and your unreverent knees,
111 [That] Make them your feet: to kneel to be forgiven
113 Whose discipline is riot. Why, even your [wars]
     hurly <in in to your obedience>
124 Should so much come too short of your great trespass
126 What country, by the nature of your error,
134 Whet their detested knives against your throats,
137 Were not all appropriate to [their] your comforts,
140 And this your momtanish inhumanity.

1 YOURSELF

146 Give up yourself to form, obey the magistrate,

1 YOURSELVES

46   Even by the rule you have among yourselves,

114

(b) General Statistics

More Addition IIc contains forty-nine speeches, nine in verse (all Sir Thomas More's, who speaks always, and alone, in verse), and forty in prose. Of its 151 lines, 92 (61%)—all More's—are in verse and 59 (39%) are in prose. More actually dominates the scene even more by rhetorical elevation and sheer articulation than these bare statistics suggest, since many of the lines in prose—following the lineation of the manuscript—are very short. Of the total 1221 words of the Addition (counted from the Concordance), 491 are different, and 26.8% of the total words are of unique occurrence. Of the different words, 164 (33.4%) are of multiple occurrence, and 327 (66.6%) occur only once. These figures bespeak finite but considerable variety.

(c) Words of Multiple Occurrence in Order of Frequency of Occurrence

As noted above, 164 words occur more than once. Of the remaining 327 that occur only once (which are not listed below), the relative frequency is .082. The columns give information as follows: (1) the total number of occurrences (absolute frequency); (2) the relative frequency; (3) the number of words occurring the same number of times; and (4) the words.

59	4.83	1	YOU				HEAR
46	3.77	1	THE				WOULD
33	2.70	1	TO	8	0.655	2	THEM
29	2.375	1·	AND				THEY
26	2.13	2	A, article	7	0.57	7	BUT, conj.
			OF				DO
17	1.39	1	YOUR				IF
15	1.23	1	IN				IT
14	1.145	1	NOT				PEACE, sb.
12	0.98	4	AS				WE
			THAT, pron.				WITH
			THEIR	6	0.49	4	HIS
			WHAT				ON
11	0.90	1	MORE, name				STRANGERS
10	0.82	7	BY				TH' (contr.)
			HAVE	5	0.41	18	ALL
			HIM				AT
			IS				BOTH
			NO				GOOD, a.
			PEACE, v.				HOW
			(interj.)				I
			WILL. v.				KING
9	0.74	5	ARE				LET's, comp. contr.
			BE				LIKE, adv.
			GOD				OUR

			PRENTICES				OBEY
			SHOULD				ONE
			SHREWSBURY				REBEL, sb.
			SHRIEVE				RULE, v.
			SURREY				SIMPLE
			THAT, conj.				SUCH
			THIS, pron.				THESE
			WHICH				THINGS
4	0.33	19	CANNOT				UPON
			COUNTRY				WERE
			DOWN				WHY
			FOR, conj.	2	0.165	61	AGAINST (+ 3 'GAINST)
			HAD				AN
			HATH				ARTHUR
			ME				AUTHORITY
			MEN				BEFORE
			MERCY				BROTHER
			MY				BUT, adv.
			NAY				BUT, prep.
			NOW				COME
			OBEDIENCE				COMMAND, v.
			OR				COULD
			POOR				COUNTRYMEN
			SAY				DEVIL
			UP				DUNG
			US				EARTH
			WE'LL				EATING
3	0.245	27	A, pron. (+ 3 HE)				ENGLAND
			ALAS				ERROR
			CAN				EVEN
			CITY				EVER
			EARL				FRIENDS
			FOR, prep.				GIVE
			'GAINST (+ 2 AGAINST)				GO
			GRANT, v.				GOT
			HE (+ 3 A, pron.)				GREAT
			HOLD, v.				HAND
			MAJESTY				INFECTED
			MAKE				KING'S, sing. poss.
			MARK, v.				LEAD, v. (lĭd)
			MARRY, interj.				LENT, v.
			MASTERS, sb.				LIFT
			NAME, sb.				LORD

MADE	THAT, a.
MAY, v.	THEN
MUCH	THERE
NOBLE, a.	THOSE
NOR	THROATS
OWN, a.	THUS
PALSEY	'TIS
SEE	TRASH, sb.
SEEK	TRUE, adv.
SELF	WARS
SHALL	WATCHINS, name
SO	WHEN
SPEAK	WISDOM
TELL	YOU'LL
THAN	

Notes:

(1) For full identification of this and other works referred to *passim*, see the list of Abbreviations (pp. 9-10).

(2) In three recent discussions, for example, Bald has argued for late 1600 and early 1601 (pp. 51-54), I. A. Shapiro for 1591-93 (*ShS*, VIII [1955], 100-105), and Jenkins for "*c.* 1590-3 for the original composition and *c.* 1594-5 for the revision" (p. 189).

(3) This is the first of four summary propositions set down in *TLS*, December 1, 1927, p. 908.

(4) Addition II*c* is an author's—presumably Shakespeare's—autograph revision of a scene earlier written by someone else. The case for its Shakespearean conception and style persuasively made by R. W. Chambers and Caroline Spurgeon makes clear that there is a fine and somewhat impractical line to be drawn here between revision and original composition; see Chambers, "The Expression of Ideas—Particularly Political Ideas—in the Three Pages, and in Shakespeare" in *Shakespeare's Hand* (pp. 142-187), and "Shakespeare and the Play of *More*" in *Man's Unconquerable Mind* (London, 1939), pp. 204-249; and Spurgeon, "Imagery in the *Sir Thomas More* Fragment" in *RES*, VI (1930), 257-270. Certainly the fragment of the original (printed as the first of the modern-spelling texts below) revised in II*c* does not show the reviser much beholden to the original for his language. Jenkins remarks that the "identification of some of the hands of the manuscript as those of well-known dramatists has led to attempts to pronounce upon *the authorship of the original version* of the play" (italics his), but "the matter is not one which promises to repay investigation" (pp. 184, 185).

(5) See "A Crux and No Crux in Hamlet I.iii: Safty:Sanctity (21) and Beguide:Beguile (131)," *ShakS*, III (1967), 43-50.

(6) My immediate obligations for assistance toward the completion of this work are great indeed. I am indebted to the Research Committee of the University of California, Los Angeles, for generous financial assistance, and to the UCLA Campus Computing Network for the use of its IBM System/360, Model 75 computer. Both for writing the programs and for making many valuable suggestions and doing his work with extraordinary intelligence and dedication I am deeply grateful to Mr. Paul D. Page, Systems Programmer for the Computing Network, whose resourcefulness and good nature I have had the good fortune to be able to draw upon for several years. Mrs. Lois Sklepowich, now a graduate student in English at the University of Virginia, keypunched

the difficult old-spelling text with patience and accuracy. The data, programs, and explanatory rubrics have been checked a number of times, and there have been several stages of reprocessing. I should like to think that everything is now in perfect order, but the complexity of the work and my own fallibility draw me up short before such a conviction; for any errors that may remain, I am responsible.

This is also the place to record that, while it was always our hope to "generalize" our programs as much as possible and to be able to make them available to others interested in processing different data for the same purposes, available funds and time prevented us from preparing the detailed "write-ups" without which the programs could probably not be "run" by anyone but the original programmer (there are also problems involved in using different computers, even of the same model, when they are of a high order of complexity).

(7) The identification of all the hands but D is based on exclusively paleographical evidence, and with S, A, C, and E "we are on unchallengeable ground. The problems are B and D" (Jenkins, p. 181). In "On Looking Over Shakespeare's 'Secretarie,'" Sergeant R. A. Huber, an expert on modern handwriting for the Royal Canadian Mounted Police, concluded, after two months' study of photographic facsimiles of D's writing and Shakespeare's six known signatures, that D's hand could not be positively identified as Shakespeare's on the basis of paleographical evidence alone; in a "Postscript," C. J. Sisson reasserts the "cumulative effect of other evidence" and the uniqueness—in his forty years' experience with manuscripts of the period—of the "spurred a" and the spelling "scilens" ("silence"); see *Stratford Papers on Shakespeare, 1960* (Toronto, 1961), pp. 52-70 and ("Postscript") 70-77.

Of the identification of hand B, Jenkins concludes that, in comparing B's work with known samples of Heywood's hand, "in view of the long time interval, it seems reasonable to give the greater weight to similarities; and there is some support from peculiarities of spelling, though here again differences have been pointed out ([by J. M. Nosworthy, "Hand B in *Sir Thomas More*," in] *The Library*, 5th series, xi. 47-50). I cannot regard the identification as improbable; but the matter is undecided" (p. 182).

(8) Bald (p. 47) says the right margin, but see the *Tudor Facsimile* and compare Greg: the eight preparatory lines were written "1-5 on original leaf, fol. 14, and 6-8 on the additional slip" (*More*, p. 89, Addition V, headnote).

(9) N.B., however, that Greg and Maunde Thompson read "THE" where I read "THE," with Bald (l. 17), and that I do not treat "IT" (l. 147b) as doubtful in the modern-spelling text or the Concordance.

(10) A disyllabic "mutines" makes rather poor, but (trisyllabic) "mutinies" good, sense. It is perhaps mildly licentious to invoke canonical Shakespeare to interpret Addition IIc, but in this case he may be taken perhaps chiefly as a witness to contemporary pronunciation. "Mutiny" is almost invariably trisyllabic in verse-contexts. "Incident" occurs three times in the plays, once certainly and once almost certainly as a disyllable, in "Their pangs of love, with other incident *throes*" and "And yet confusion live! *Plagues* incident to men" (New Arden *Tim.* V.i.199 and IV.i.21), and all three times in similar verbal contexts; N.B. italicized words in *Tim.* and cf. "a *malady* / Most incident to maids" (New Arden *WT* IV.iv.124-125).

(11) In l. 28 R. W. Chambers also modernizes as "Peace, ho! Peace!"; see *Man's Unconquerable Mind* (London, 1939), p. 221. Of *momtanish* in l. 140 Greg writes: "There is here no dispute as to the reading; the original is perfectly clear, and the editors are agreed that there are but three minims between the *o* and the *t*. The only question is what the writer intended. To print 'momtanish' no doubt implies slightly more than the original warrants, but to print 'mountanish' is to approach conjectural emendation. I fear the interpretations 'momtanish, mawmtanish, Mahometanish,' and 'mountanish, mountainish' are about equally unsatisfactory. Were the manuscript a copy, one might indulge in all manner of conjecture, but, it being autograph, the choice is

118

uncomfortably restricted" (*TLS*, November 7, 1919, p. 630; to the same purpose in *IMD*, p. 214, l. 156n). The headword is "MOMTANISH."

(12) Giles E. Dawson and Laetitia Kennedy-Skipton, *Elizabethan Handwriting 1500-1650: A Manual* (New York, 1966), p. 19.

(13) In slightly more detail (based on Paul Page's description), "sorting" is accomplished in terms of ten fields: (1) subject-letter; (2) position of subject-letter (solitary through terminal); (3) class of subject-letter (in the order capital, lower-case, superscript); (4) letter to the left of the subject-letter, in a field three characters long, with standard alphabetic characters placed at the left followed by two blanks (blank $=\wedge$), and special characters converted for sorting thus: $@ = ER_\wedge$, $p = PAR$, $\wp = PRO$, $\neg = S_{\wedge\wedge}$, $^c = C1_\wedge$, $^h = H1_\wedge$, $^r = R1_\wedge$, $^u = U1_\wedge$, $^t = T1_\wedge$, $\tilde{o} = O2_\wedge$, $\tilde{t} = T2_\wedge$, and $ff = F_{\wedge\wedge}$; since blanks sort before other characters, $@$ follows E but precedes F, and c follows C but precedes D, for example; (5) letter to the right of the subject-letter, as with the letter to the left; (6) characters other than the subject-letter and the first letter on either side of it, which are converted to a single alphabetic character for sorting thus: $@ = E$, $p = P$, $\wp = P$, $\neg = S$, $^c = C$, $^h = H$, $^r = R$, $^u = U$, $^t = T$, $\hat{o} = O$, $\tilde{t} = T$, and $ff = F$; (8) capitals, when not the subject-letter, which take precedence over the same lower-case non-subject-letter; (9) underscored letters, which follow the same letters not underscored; (10) line-number. For sorting purposes, all letters are treated as lower-case, and sorting in terms of capitalization is accomplished by fields 3 and 8.

(14) See Chambers, *Man's Unconquerable Mind*, p. 228. Since modern *on* and *one* are both spelled *on* throughout the Addition, the intention in the manuscript is ambiguous, but "One supposition" seems to me somewhat less likely than "On," because More goes on (in l. 91) with "First, 'tis a sin," apparently to begin a series of suppositions (collective in "on supposition"), which, however, he abandons, inferentially to pursue the hint of an interruption by "All" in line 96. Moreover (to invoke strictly canonical works, though chiefly to illustrate an idiomatic usage), "in," at least, is used with "supposition" in *MV* I.iii.18 and *Err.* III.ii.50, where "in that glorious supposition" is used in a collective sense. But there is confusion elsewhere in the Addition, and I am by no means certain that *on* and not *one* was intended.

(15) *RES*, VII (1931), 67-69; see other references cited by Bald and also J. M. Nosworthy, "Shakespeare and *Sir Thomas More*," *RES*, n.s., VI (1955), 12-25, esp. 17ff.

(16) Two miswritings—*ar* (ll. 35 and 107)—and an intralineal stage-direction (*all*, l. 38) have been excluded from the Concordance but not from the counts in the Frequency List.